THE EVERYTHING
FATHER-TO-BE BOOK
2ND EDITION

Dear Reader,

Let me welcome you to the second edition of *The Everything® Father-to-Be Book: A Survival Guide for Men*. Mark Twain said that "a classic" was a book that everyone admired but no one read. Well, I am happy to say that new fathers, fathers-to-be, and lots of others have turned *The Everything® Father-to-Be-Book* into a parenting classic that people not only admire, but read as well. I am very grateful for that.

While the first edition helped guide tens of thousands of fathers-to-be along the sometimes bumpy road to fatherhood, this new and improved second edition contains all the features of the first plus new ones for adoptive parents, more advice on money and jobs, updates on health, environmental, and emotional issues, and more coping strategies for dads and moms after the newborn comes home. In addition, there are more than thirty "Parent to Parent" sidebars—practical tips for new fathers-to-be from parents who have been in the childhood trenches and really know what they're talking about.

As a father of four and the author of many articles and books on parenting, most geared toward men, I wish you only the best in this grand adventure you are embarking on. Be sure to drop me a line and keep me posted on your progress at KevinNelsonWriter.com.

Kevin Nelson

Welcome to the EVERYTHING® Series!

These handy, accessible books give you all you need to tackle a difficult project, gain a new hobby, comprehend a fascinating topic, prepare for an exam, or even brush up on something you learned back in school but have since forgotten.

You can choose to read an *Everything*® book from cover to cover or just pick out the information you want from our four useful boxes: e-questions, e-facts, e-alerts, and e-ssentials.

We give you everything you need to know on the subject, but throw in a lot of fun stuff along the way, too.

We now have more than 400 *Everything*® books in print, spanning such wide-ranging categories as weddings, pregnancy, cooking, music instruction, foreign language, crafts, pets, New Age, and so much more. When you're done reading them all, you can finally say you know *Everything*®!

QUESTION

Answers to common questions

ESSENTIAL

Important snippets of information

ALERT

Urgent warnings

FACT

Quick handy tips

QUOTE

Advice and insights from parents who've been there

PUBLISHER Karen Cooper

DIRECTOR OF ACQUISITIONS AND INNOVATION Paula Munier

MANAGING EDITOR, EVERYTHING® SERIES Lisa Laing

COPY CHIEF Casey Ebert

ACQUISITIONS EDITOR Brett Palana-Shanahan

SENIOR DEVELOPMENT EDITOR Brett Palana-Shanahan

EDITORIAL ASSISTANT Hillary Thompson

EVERYTHING® SERIES COVER DESIGNER Erin Alexander

LAYOUT DESIGNERS Colleen Cunningham, Elisabeth Lariviere, Ashley Vierra, Denise Wallace

Visit the entire Everything® series at *www.everything.com*

THE
EVERYTHING®
FATHER-TO-BE BOOK

2ND EDITION

A survival guide for men

Kevin Nelson

Avon, Massachusetts

This book is dedicated to fathers everywhere.

An Everything® Series Book.
Everything® and everything.com® are registered trademarks of F+W Media, Inc.

Published by Adams Media, a division of F+W Media, Inc.
57 Littlefield Street, Avon, MA 02322 U.S.A.
www.adamsmedia.com

ISBN 10: 1-4405-0460-1
ISBN 13: 978-1-4405-0460-0
eISBN 10: 1-4405-0461-X
eISBN 13: 978-1-4405-0461-7

Printed in the United States of America.

10 9 8 7 6 5 4 3 2 1

Library of Congress Cataloging-in-Publication Data
is available from the publisher.

Illustrations by Eulala Conner.

*This book is available at quantity discounts for bulk purchases.
For information, please call 1-800-289-0963.*

Contents

Acknowledgments

A book, like a family, is never the product of a single person, and this is certainly true in this case. First, let me thank Brett Palana-Shanahan, my editor, and Adams Media for their commitment to new fathers and fathers-to-be by releasing this newly revised and expanded second edition of *The Everything® Father-to-Be Book: A Survival Guide for Men.*

I wish to thank my wife, Jennifer, who makes me a better man. I also wish to dedicate this book to my children, Annie, Hank, Gabriel, and Leah. They teach me how to be a better parent every day. I would be remiss not to mention my own parents, Delmar and Frances Nelson. They gave me love and taught me about the importance of faith and humor and loyalty and giving—qualities that never go out of style and that I hope my children learn from me.

Top Ten Things Every Father-to-Be Should Know

1. How to keep your relationship with your partner and your sex life thriving, active, and fun during pregnancy.

2. What to say—and what not to say—about your partner's changing body and other potentially touchy pregnancy issues.

3. How to be the world's greatest labor coach.

4. How to keep your sanity when your parents, her parents, aunts, uncles, and other family members descend on you.

5. All about job and workplace issues, including strategies on how to get paid time off when the baby arrives.

6. Why you can relax about fainting in the delivery room (it won't happen).

7. Tips on how to keep the money coming in while balancing your work and job with your new responsibilities as a father.

8. How to be a hero to your partner when she's feeling low, sick, scared, and in pain during labor.

9. How to cope with all the changes, emotional and otherwise, that are occurring in your life.

10. How to minimize the stress and maximize the enjoyment of having a baby.

Introduction

It has been said that that being a father is the most important thing most men will ever do in their lives. Only a few select individuals will be President of the United States or rescue a stranded family from a burning building or sink the winning basket with time running out in the seventh game of the NBA finals. But many men will become fathers, giving them the opportunity to become everyday heroes to their children.

This second edition of *The Everything® Father-to-Be Book* is intended for new fathers and fathers-to-be. It is designed to guide the new father through the ups and downs of pregnancy, taking him all the way through to the birth of his child and the days and weeks after he brings his son or daughter home for the first time. While the focus is on first-timers, there is plenty of solid information here for second- and third-time fathers who may need a refresher course on how to be a labor coach, how to introduce the new child to siblings, and other baby-related issues.

Many men are not sure what to think when they learn, for the first time, that they are going to become a father. Panic is one reaction. Another is, "How can this be happening to me?" After the initial anxiety passes, many new fathers get totally into it. They become curious about this new thing they have never experienced and they want to learn more.

Not all new fathers are like this, of course. Some are more reluctant participants. Because the baby is developing inside their partner's body, and not theirs, they may feel uninvolved or cut off from what's going on. These men may have to go through the birth itself and see the baby before they finally feel connected to the drama that has been unfolding around them for the previous nine months. The goal of this book is to speak to all types of new fathers—those who are into it from the get-go and those who may need a little nudging here and there—and to introduce all of them to the wonder of this experience.

Men tend to be mission-oriented. Give us a job and we will go out and do it. The problem that some new fathers have with pregnancy is that they are not sure what to do or what their job is. This book will show you the jobs that you can do during this time, including, most importantly perhaps, how you can support your partner.

Ah, but there's the rub. This may be an unfamiliar position for many men. They may not be accustomed to playing second fiddle in their family. But interestingly, a man shows leadership by supporting his partner and the life developing inside her. He recognizes that something is happening that is larger than himself, and he does some growing up during this period. He becomes a father.

Nothing physical happens inside the body of the man during pregnancy (although some do feel sympathy pains when their partners are going through morning sickness), and yet he is being asked to make the journey from not being a father to being a father. Is it any wonder that some men stumble along the way? Fathers-to-be experience emotions they've never had before—fear of fainting in the delivery room, worry about the health of the baby, money pressures, concern over how a child will affect their relationship with their partners—and they're not quite sure how to handle them. Some are embarrassed that they have these emotions at all.

For new fathers and their partners, pregnancy is a trip into a vast, unexplored territory. And just like any good adventurer exploring the unknown, you will need to have the right tools. Let this book serve as your compass and map as you discover the new world of fatherhood—and become an everyday hero to your family.

CHAPTER 1

The New World of Fatherhood

It is a brand new world for fathers today. Becoming a father today is a far different enterprise than it was for your father when you were born. These changes bring greater challenges and responsibilities for men, but they also offer immense rewards and joys. This chapter will prepare you for the road ahead and what to expect along the way.

Becoming a Father

To state the obvious, being a father is different from being a mother. You have a different role in the family and a different job to do. You see things differently than your partner does, and you will have a different relationship with your child than she does.

Some of the most crucial differences between a father and a mother become obvious during pregnancy. The most dramatic, and visible, changes occur with the woman. Her body changes as the baby grows inside her, and a whole host of emotions accompany these physical changes.

A father, on the other hand, is an entirely different breed of cat. Although some men experience sympathy pains and other physical symptoms, virtually nothing happens directly to the man. His body does not expand and change. He's the same fella he always was—except that now he is about to have a little rug rat crawling around the house.

ALERT

The Internet is a boundless source of information that can help answer specific questions that arise. Some of this information is reliable; much of it is not. On medical issues involving pregnancy, it is always best to follow a physician's advice and your own common sense rather than any advice you may find on the web (or anywhere else, for that matter).

The unique challenge that men face is that they must come to terms with becoming a father almost entirely on an emotional level, rather than a physical one. The good news for today's fathers-to-be is that they have an unprecedented level of support and a wide variety of resources available to them. Some of those resources include the following:

- This book and others like it that speak to men
- Father and parenting websites on the Internet
- Fathering blogs, social network sites, and online discussion forums
- Other fathers
- Men's and fathers' support groups
- Your partner, her family, and yours

These and other resources are potentially useful to men, and they will be discussed in greater detail later in this book. It is important for new fathers to realize that they are not alone as they embark on this journey.

QUOTE

"No one ever tells expectant fathers how much fun it is going to be," said Gary Grillo, father of two girls. "Well, it is. If you let it, this will be the most fun you have ever had in your life. Everything is worth it the first time she looks at you—not to mention the first time you hear her say 'Dadda.'"

Greater Expectations, Greater Rewards

More is expected of fathers today than ever before. You are still expected to be a good provider, but that's not the end of your responsibilities. You are also expected to actively participate in the birth of your child and to take a hands-on approach in raising him or her. Additionally, your partner expects you to always be there for her in a loving, nurturing way.

It's a lot to handle, no? At times it may seem overwhelming. But fatherhood is a job and, like any job, it helps to know what your duties are and how you fit in. Here, then, is a general job description for being a father.

Job One: Provider/Protector

Despite all the ways that fatherhood has changed over the years, your primary role is the same as it was for the cavemen and for every father since then. You need to provide for your family, and it's your job to protect them to make sure they are safe. The mother's primary focus will be inward, on the baby. Yours will be on creating a safe, secure place to raise your child.

Men are hard-wired for this job; it is not something that you will need to go to school to learn. Often, the first thoughts a man has when he learns his partner is pregnant are these: "How am I going to pay for this? Do I need to work more? What do I need to do to make this happen?"

All men have these thoughts or similar ones. They are normal and natural, an instinctive reaction to the promise and responsibility of childbirth.

Being a provider is one of the most fundamental ways you can help your partner and child.

Job Two: Participant

One of the biggest jobs a father has is as a birth coach, a responsibility that will be discussed in greater detail later. But being a birth coach is only one aspect of a larger requirement for fathers today. They are expected to participate in all areas of family and household life. This is in part due to the fact that many women are themselves working outside the home, and these mothers need more help with the baby from their partners.

Being asked to participate more may seem like a negative because you feel like you are getting pulled in lots of different directions at the same time. It is ultimately a positive thing, though. since with greater responsibilities come greater rewards. Since you are around your child more—changing diapers, feeding her, taking her for walks—you develop a closer relationship with her. Every father wants that.

Birth and health care specialists say that one of the biggest worries of fathers-to-be is that they will faint during their child's birth. Many men have seen movies or television shows in which the father collapses comically in the delivery room. The fact is that this almost never happens; virtually no men faint during childbirth.

Job Three: Support Person and Nurturer

A vital part of being a father is supporting your partner because by supporting her, you support your child. Having a good relationship with your partner is the best thing the two of you can do for your child. Some fathers-to-be may be uncomfortable with this job because it represents a change in the way you perceive yourself and your role as a man. Putting your partner's needs ahead of yours is an important part of showing your commitment—to both your partner and your future child.

You may come into a rough patch where you lose your job or the money isn't flowing in the way you wish. But you can still be there for your partner in valuable ways that have nothing to do with making a living. First and foremost, listen to her. Let her talk about her feelings, and try to listen without judging or criticizing. Demonstrate that she can confide in you about the sometimes scary changes that are happening inside her.

Birth Then and Now

People have been having babies since, well, since the beginning of people. But the childbirth process has changed dramatically over the years. These changes have largely come about through advances in medical technology that make it safer than ever before to have a baby. Although there are still dangers in childbirth, for both the mother and the baby, the risks are significantly lower than they were in previous generations.

The Way It Used to Be

For centuries, almost all births took place at home. Childbirth was regarded as the exclusive domain of women. Usually only females were present, including a midwife who assisted in the delivery. Fathers rarely participated, nor were they expected to.

The mortality rate was far higher than it is today. Sometimes the baby or the mother died during childbirth. Because it involved creation, the act of having a child was imbued with mystery. Ritual and superstition entered into it, and the midwife, who was not medically trained, often oversaw these mysterious rites.

Childbirth as a Medical Procedure

In more recent generations, the hospital replaced the home as the primary place to have a baby. Anesthesia came into use, which required a doctor's involvement. Additionally, people began to feel that a hospital with physicians, nurses, and trained medical specialists in attendance was the best environment for both mother and child.

Once hospitals and doctors got into the act, the process of having a baby underwent a major transformation. Where it had once been seen as an act of creation fraught with danger and mystery, childbirth came to be regarded as a medical procedure similar to surgery. Mom was, in fact, placed on a surgical table, her feet resting in stirrups. She received medication to numb the pain, and the operation proceeded.

One element of childbirth that did not change from earlier times, however, was the role of dear old Dad. Just as in earlier days, he was the odd man out. Most of the time you could find him in the waiting room, nervously pacing the floor and making jokes with the other men there. When the baby arrived, he brought flowers to Mom (still not a bad idea) and handed out cigars.

Birth Today

The experience of giving birth today is radically different than it was for your parents or grandparents. Hospitals and their labor and delivery procedures have changed in recent decades. In part, this is a response to couples who have insisted on more involvement for the father and less of a "surgical" feel to the birth experience.

You will want, of course, the best physicians and medical services available to you. Even if you choose not to use it in every case, you will probably like the idea of having the latest technology at your disposal, especially if a crisis occurs. And you will want information about all of your options, including pain-killing drugs (again, even if your partner opts not to use them).

In a famous incident in the last decade, David Williams, a tackle with the Houston Oilers, skipped a National Football League game to attend the birth of his son. The Oilers reacted by fining Williams and threatening to suspend him, causing a national uproar. Since then, almost every occupation, including professional sports, recognizes the right of a father to attend the birth of a child.

But if you are like nearly all couples these days, you want your child's birth to be more than a purely medical event. Some couples may decide not to have their baby in a hospital, but rather to stage the delivery at home. Those at a hospital nevertheless want to birth their baby in a setting that resembles home—a place that is quiet, comfortable, and relaxed. Whatever "blend" of old and new you and your partner choose, the two of you are sure to be making lots of decisions over the next months—more decisions, perhaps, than you have ever made together before.

Dad as Birth Coach

From the onset of pregnancy to birth and beyond, this generation of dads is more actively involved with their children than any other in history.

An overwhelming percentage of fathers serve as birth coach for their partner. They look forward to this challenge and rise to the responsibilities it entails. Giving birth is not a "woman's matter" anymore. Men accept that they are part of the deal, too, and for the most part they are happy to be one of the first faces welcoming their babies into the world.

These facts notwithstanding, a man's place in this brave new world is still not secure. Hospitals and physicians often pay lip service to the importance of fathers, but then disregard them or treat them like a fifth wheel. Some (though almost certainly not your partner) may see you as a spectator to this process, irrelevant even.

Along with the negativity you may encounter from the medical profession and others are your own feelings of uncertainty and possible incompetence. You may not feel comfortable in a medical setting. You may not understand everything about a woman's body—what man does?—and your questions may seem crude and stupid. All this may make you wonder if you are up to the task ahead.

You owe it to at least three people to fight through the negativity and doubts and keep going. The first is your partner, who needs you by her side. The second is your growing child who, it has been shown, learns to distinguish his mother's and father's voices while still in the womb. Last but not least is you. Being present for the birth of your child is without a doubt one of the most flat-out amazing experiences you will ever have. You don't want to miss it.

QUOTE

"Just stick with it and don't sweat the small stuff," Mike Maggart, father of three, says to new fathers and fathers-to-be. "There are no hard-and-fast rules for a lot of these issues, and if there are, they change back and forth with time anyhow. Everyone makes mistakes. Becky and I did what we always thought was best for the kids and the situation. You will, too."

A Different Role for You

While being a birth coach is important, it is nonetheless secondary to the bigger job that your partner is doing. She is the one who is birthing the baby and doing the real, hard, painful work. Most men are glad not to be in that position once they see their partners going through so much agony.

Still, it points out a central fact: you are not the central player in this drama. Baby and Mom come first, and you are a distant third. This may be an unfamiliar position for you, but being a father in today's world means that you must learn and adapt to new roles for yourself.

A Supporting Role

As mentioned, you are not the lead actor in this drama; your partner and baby are. The job of a supporting actor is just that—to support the lead players. Your job is essentially to make the star of the show—the mother of your child—feel good and keep her performing. If you do that, you will be doing your job. And there is great satisfaction in this.

In the later months of pregnancy, you will take childbirth preparation classes. These classes focus principally on Mom. As her coach, you are there to learn techniques to support her, both physically and emotionally, when she goes into labor. Again, while this is a valuable role to play, it is still a supporting one.

An Advisory Role

One of the vital roles that a man plays during pregnancy, and especially during childbirth, is that of advisor. You are going to advise your partner on lots of issues. Some advice she will heed; some of it she will ignore. So it goes.

Ultimately, though, your partner will make the final call, not you. Most men accept this and have no problem with it. They trust her instincts, especially in matters concerning her own body, and are willing to play second fiddle in this regard.

A Decision-Making Role

In the throes of labor, however, a woman may be unable to make decisions for herself. She may be out of her mind with pain. That is where you sometimes have to step in, assess the situation based on the advice of doctors, nurses, and others, and make tough, on-the-spot decisions.

These decisions affect not only you, but your partner and your baby, too. Whatever role you happen to be playing at any given moment, when you make a decision, you will now have to consider its impact on your family. Get used to it. That is what it means to be a father.

ALERT

The responsibility for making decisions during labor and delivery never falls solely on the shoulders of the birth coach. Physicians, nurses, and the nurse-midwife provide counsel and can and will intervene if necessary. A friend or a member of your partner's family may be present as well. You can also hire a professional labor assistant to give advice.

Adoptive Fathers and Other Types of Dads

"There are many ways to create a family," said attorney and mother Brette McWhorter Sember, and no truer words were ever spoken. There are all sorts of families and all sorts of ways that men become fathers.

One way is through adoption. You and your partner may have adopted (or are adopting) a child from this country or another. If that describes you, you know that this process can be complicated and expensive. Almost certainly an agency or service has assisted you in this quest.

You may also be having a child through nontraditional but increasingly common methods such as artificial insemination or surrogate motherhood. The goal is the same in every case: to have a child, to raise a child, and to make the child part of a loving, caring family.

A dad is a dad is a dad. No matter what path you have taken to get here, you are becoming part of the club too. The fundamental rules apply to you as well: your partner needs you, your child will need you, and the ground underneath you will be shifting rapidly and constantly.

The Changes Ahead

It is true that having a baby changes everything. These changes reach into all the major departments of your life and the minor ones too. These changes begin virtually as soon as you hear her say, "Um, honey, you know what? I think I missed my period."

After you pick yourself up off the floor, there is no reason to panic. Take a few deep breaths, and smile. Give her a big kiss. The biggest rollercoaster ride of your lives is now beginning. Following are three key areas of your life that will start to go up and down, and down and up.

Your Relationship

Changes may have already occurred in this department, depending on how far along your partner is in her pregnancy. You may find that she has less time and attention for you. She may not have as much interest in sex as she once did. She may be extremely tired or experiencing morning sickness. She may experience emotional highs and lows that you have trouble keeping up with at times.

There's no denying that a baby (even one still in the womb) creates stresses and strains on a couple. When both parties are willing, however, this time can become a golden opportunity to grow together as a couple—and still have fun and a wonderful time in bed!

Your Job and Career

Changes will most certainly occur in the professional realm once you find out you're having a baby. Both you and your employer may suddenly regard each other in a different light.

For example, you may work long hours or travel frequently in your job but, with a baby on the way, you may not want to be away quite so much from your partner. When the baby comes, you may want to be home still more. Your changed view toward your job may in turn cause your employer to reassess your place and standing in the company.

FACT

Studies have shown that becoming a father can help a man in his work life. Feeling the need to provide for his family makes him work harder, and this spurs him on to greater accomplishments and a better career. Having a baby also teaches patience, perseverance, and other lessons that can improve on-the-job performance.

Your View of the World

The biggest change in your life when you become a father is the change that occurs in your outlook. Your attitude about things, your view of the world, shifts and expands. You no longer look at things in quite the same way you did before.

This change in attitude does not occur overnight. It comes on slowly, over time. Pregnancy covers three quarters of a year, which gives you ample time to come to terms with the idea of little ol' you becoming Dear Ol' Dad.

Of course, your partner may have an entirely different view—about the length of a pregnancy, that is. She is, after all, the one who is carrying Junior around inside her. And Junior keeps getting bigger and bigger. By the ninth month or so she is going to be quite sick of the whole business and ready to pop that baby out.

Learning to be a father is one of the simplest things a man can do—and one of the hardest and most complicated. There are great expectations and challenges for fathers today, along with great joys and rewards.

CHAPTER 2

Conception and Pregnancy

Fatherhood begins at the moment of conception. After this moment comes the crazy, apple-cart-upsetting knowledge that, yes, you are indeed going to have a baby. What do you do when you first hear the news? What steps do you take at home and at work? This chapter gives you the lowdown.

Planned and Unplanned

The majority of pregnancies are unplanned. Even if they are planned, they are unplanned in the sense that you never know until you're pregnant that you are. They almost always come as a surprise to both Mom and Dad. Surprise may, in fact, be too mild a word. Both of you may feel at first like you have just been hit over the head with a baseball bat.

Conception is a simple yet mysterious process. Some couples may have been trying hard to have a baby, stopped for a while because they were unsuccessful, and then suddenly and inexplicably got pregnant. Others may have caught lightning in a bottle and conceived a child the first weekend they made love after stopping birth control. Some may have gotten pregnant while on the pill or another form of contraception.

Ultimately, the genesis of your pregnancy does not matter. What matters is the fact that both of you are bringing a new life into the world.

FACT

A man ejaculates between 200 and 400 million sperm during an orgasm. Only some of these sperm survive the journey up the womb to the promised land of a woman's fallopian tubes. Once the sperm enters the egg, the door is shut and no other sperm can get in. The instantaneous fusion of sperm and egg forms the single cell in which life begins.

Hearing the News

After he plants the seed, a man basically loses control of the gestation process. The woman is the one who carries the baby, the one whose internal processes will transform that single cell into a fully formed, amazingly complex little human being with eyes, ears, nose, lips, skin, and maybe even some cute fluffy wisps of hair just like Dad's.

Your partner will be the first to know about her possible pregnancy. It does not matter if it was planned or not. In every case, she will know or suspect something is different before you see any signs because she will have missed her period. In some cases, she may even have proceeded without you—received medical confirmation of her pregnancy from a blood or urine test—before she lets you in on her secret.

This puts you into a reactive position. She is going to be telling you the news, even if it is still preliminary, and you are going to be on the receiving end. The emotions you may feel when you hear this news for the first time are worth exploring.

Shock

Learning that you are about to have a baby, if you were not expecting it, is shocking news. Even if you were planning and hoping for it, this information can still catch you off guard. You may feel stunned and completely blown away. "What?" you say. "Are you sure?" Before fully accepting the news, many men need to see the results of a pregnancy test. A test provides outside verification beyond the simple fact that your partner may have missed her period.

Fear and Worry

After your immediate shock fades, more emotions will follow. You may feel all of these things at once, or they may come on over time. All of what you feel falls under the category of "normal and natural." Every father-to-be experiences these emotions at one time or another.

You do not know what to expect because you have never done this before. People can tell you what it is like, but that is not the same thing as actually living it and experiencing it for yourself. Until you do, feelings of worry and unease will probably always be at the back of your mind.

Sadness

Sadness or even depression can come over you in your quieter moments after learning you are about to become a father. While a woman feels as if she is gaining something in having a child, many men experience an opposite reaction; they may experience feelings of loss.

You may be asking yourself, "Is my partner going to get so wrapped up in the baby that she forgets about me? Am I going to lose her? Is having a baby going to hurt our relationship?" These questions and more will be discussed in Chapter 6.

Excitement

Emotions, being emotions, are hard to predict. They do not follow a predictable pattern. If you do not feel these exact emotions right away, that is perfectly okay. Every man is entitled to his own emotional response; there are no "shoulds" here. Of course, if you do not feel anything at all upon hearing the news you are going to be a father, it may mean that you lack a pulse. Better call the doctor because possibly you are no longer alive.

QUOTE

"After getting over the immediate shock of 'How did this happen?'" says Rich Freedman, father of a son, "you can then think of what's important about being a parent: surviving the next eighteen years." Rich also has advice for coping with your partner's morning sickness: "Stock up on pickles, ice cream, and a really good sedative."

Once you get over the initial shock, you will certainly feel excited at some point. It is possible, however, that your partner's initial excitement may surpass your own. She may be bubbly as champagne while you feel flat. The reverse may be true too—you may feel elated, but she may feel like the world just fell on top of her. Whatever is going on inside your head, you will need to deal in some way with her feelings.

Your Job Begins: Reassuring Her

It is worth noting that, even in the murky world of emotions, the laws of science still apply. Sir Isaac Newton's famous third law of motion reads, "For every action, there is an equal and opposite reaction." Every careful man understands that when his partner first says those fateful words to him, "Honey, I'm pregnant," your reaction is fundamental. Her initial feelings about this surprising development in your lives will be influenced, to some degree, by what you say and how you react.

Men are not robots. You are going to have an emotional response to this breathtaking news. What may help you, though, is a little understanding of what your partner is going through at this moment. She is going to be all over the map emotionally, surging with feelings that are similar to (but frequently different than) yours. The following are some examples:

- Excitement over having a baby of her own
- Worry over what you are thinking and how you may react
- Anxiety over what this may mean for your relationship
- Uncertainty because she has so many questions that need answers
- Concern that during the weeks she did not know she was pregnant she has somehow unintentionally harmed the baby's health
- Fear about the pain of childbirth that she has heard so many stories about
- Relief that something she has perhaps wanted for some time has finally come to pass

Emotions are coursing through both of you like raging rivers. You have a great deal to talk about. These early moments can be intensely meaningful in the life of a young couple, and yet they also carry potential risk. Above all, your partner needs to know that, no matter what, you are in this together and that you will love her and stand by her.

The Home Pregnancy Test

A home pregnancy test is a commercial product that can provide a preliminary assessment of whether or not your partner is bearing a child. There are many different brands available at drugstores, supermarkets, and online that retail for $10 to $20. Most couples cannot resist the temptation to run down to the store and pick one up to see if what they suspect may actually be true.

FACT

Home pregnancy tests claim to have an almost foolproof accuracy rate. However, one independent study showed that one in four home urine tests produced a false negative. Keep in mind that a number of factors (including even what brand test you're using) can affect how soon after conception you can get a reliable positive response from the test.

For best results, a woman should wait several days after her menstrual cycle has run its course to make sure she is not jumping the gun. You almost assuredly know nothing about the timing of your partner's monthly cycle. As with so many other things having to do with pregnancy, you will have to rely on her.

Your partner will almost certainly perform the test herself. It involves collecting a urine sample, and while you may see yourself as involved and supportive, you do not want to be *that* involved. When she is done, you can inspect the results together, although they are sometimes hard to read. A colored line forms on the test strip that indicates whether or not a fertilized egg is present in the uterine wall. Sometimes this line will be too light to read and you may have to try again.

The Blood Test

Pregnancy can be detected as early as one week after conception. Since there is still a margin of error, however slim, associated with a home pregnancy test, its results cannot be considered conclusive. Some couples may skip it altogether to get a definitive answer right away. The way to do that is with a blood test.

The blood test is considered "the gold standard" of pregnancy tests. It can be done at a doctor's office or a laboratory. Just a few drops of her blood will tell you what you need to know. It may take a day or two, but the results will be accurate—you won't need to worry about a false negative or positive.

ESSENTIAL

The news of a baby on the way is cause for celebration. Buy your partner flowers or a nice gift. Treat yourselves to a special dinner, or go on a date to the beach or a park. Or don't do anything—just hang at home and giggle and talk about what is past, passing, and to come.

If your partner suspects she is pregnant but isn't sure, it is important for her to get checked out as soon as possible. She needs to see a doctor who can give her an internal exam (and also perhaps administer the blood test). Once you know for certain, you can start moving forward with the various things that need to be done.

Looking Ahead to the Due Date

Two questions immediately pop into the minds of most parents-to-be when they learn they are pregnant: "Is it a boy or girl?" and "When will he or she arrive?" The doctor will be able to calculate the due date for you.

From conception to birth, pregnancy normally lasts anywhere from thirty-eight to forty-two weeks, which, if you do the math, is not nine months. It is more like nine months and change, or even ten months. Some babies come early, some come late. Very few of them arrive when they are supposed to or according to your carefully thought-out plans.

A due date makes this whole business of having a baby seem a little more real, especially for men. The growing embryo is immediately a real and active presence for your partner because, ready or not, changes are occurring in her body. Not so with a man. Being able to flip to a page on a calendar and note the day in July or September or January helps make the process seem a little less abstract.

Be careful, though, about revealing the date to in-laws, relatives, and friends. It is better to be on the vague side—tell them the due month, perhaps, rather than the actual day. The reason for this is that if people know the date, as it gets closer and closer, they will start calling you to ask, "Has it happened yet?" However well meaning they may be, you and especially your partner do not need (and will not want) that sort of pressure at that time.

Calculating the due date is an inexact science. It is done for the benefit of adults, and babies pay no attention to it. It is the rare child who actually arrives punctually on his due date. Most, however, are born within two weeks of this day.

What Happens Now?

After about five or six weeks of life, the embryo inside your partner's body—your baby—is about the size of an apple seed. Despite his tiny size, he has already formed a simple brain and has begun to develop the beginnings of a spine, blood vessels, and a central nervous system. His itty-bitty heart is starting to beat. Although he has grown like gangbusters in a very short time, he still has a long way to go before he is ready to come out.

This is a good thing—a great thing. It gives you time to plan, and to absorb some of what you have been feeling. You do not need to know everything right away. You will learn what you need to know, and you can figure out all the things that need to be figured out in time.

But there are some things you need to jump on right out of the chute. Your partner needs to schedule an appointment with an obstetrician, or baby doctor, if she has not already done so. Make plans to go with her. She needs to start taking prenatal vitamins. A gentle reminder from you until she gets into the habit might be nice.

ALERT

Physicians strongly urge pregnant women to stop or reduce certain habits because of their potential harm to the baby. These include smoking, drinking alcohol, using recreational drugs, and drinking caffeinated beverages. Your partner should avoid taking antibiotics or over-the-counter drugs until she speaks to her doctor.

Your partner will naturally take more interest in her pregnancy than you do because it directly affects her body. Because of her self-interest, instincts, and passion, and because you may not feel entirely comfortable discussing female body issues, you may be inclined to step back and let her take charge. This strategy works well enough to a point. A better approach is to show support for your partner at this vulnerable early stage by being involved from the get-go. In health matters especially, you can influence her and indirectly promote the welfare of that hard-charging, hard-working kid you are helping to bring into the world.

Sharing the News

Every newly pregnant couple faces the question of whom to tell and when. It's a pleasant sort of dilemma. As with so many things during this time, there is no right or wrong approach. There is only the way that you, as a couple, choose to do it and what works for both of you.

Some couples take a cautious approach, preferring to wait to tell people until after three months or so have passed. After this point, the threat of miscarriage drops sharply. The greatest risk of miscarriage is in the first twelve weeks of pregnancy (although it can still occur later). These couples prefer not to tell people the good news and then, if something happens, have to follow this up with bad news. They wait until they're confident all is right with the baby and things are going swimmingly and then reveal the happy news.

Other couples are less cautious. They see no reason to wait, and they eagerly share the good news virtually as soon as they know it themselves. The pleasure in telling people immediately far outweighs the small risk of burdening them with disappointment later. Then there are those who are just not good at keeping a secret. An accidental slip of the tongue arouses a sibling's curiosity, and, before you know it, the whole family knows.

Telling Family and Friends

Some people you are going to want to tell in person, some over the phone, and others with an e-mail blast or by posting it on Facebook. Heck, if you're on Twitter, why not send out a tweet too? If your parents or in-laws live close by, it is a nice gesture to pay them a visit to reveal the news in person. If they live too far away to do that, a phone call will do the trick. If your partner calls her parents, be sure to get on the phone with them too. As you'll see, her parents and yours (assuming they're all around and able to help) can play a very useful role both before and after the baby is born.

One advantage of a group e-mail or Facebook post is that you can tell a whole bunch of people at once, if you wish. These people may not be super-close friends of yours, but you still want them to know the news. They can respond to your posting with their comments, and everyone in your extended social group can feel part of this big moment.

If you have a regular group of guys you play poker with or hang with, tell them in person. Expect some good-natured ribbing about how you are going to be knee-deep in diapers and one of the walking wounded from lack of sleep and all that. This might be a good time to spring for a bottle of Johnny Walker Gold Label and a box of Macanudo cigars and experience some old-fashioned male bonding.

Reactions That May Surprise You

You probably don't have to worry when you break the news to your buddies. They are going to offer congrats, make some jokes, and then tell you to shut up and deal the cards. But with other people, particularly family members, you may be surprised at their reaction. It may not be what you expected from them.

Although you may be spilling over with excitement, your parents may be instantly shocked into silence or a studied detachment. Remember your surprise when your partner told you she had missed her period? Well, the news may deliver a similar blow to your folks and in-laws. This represents a big event in their lives, too, and it may take them a little time to absorb it all. Some grandparents-to-be aren't thrilled about becoming grandparents, at least not initially. It represents a big life shift for them too.

This may be true not just for family but friends as well, including your poker-playing buddies. Although they may make jokes, privately one or two may wonder how the baby is going to affect your friendship with them, just as you wonder how it is going to affect your relationship with your partner. One of those guys may have been trying to get pregnant with his wife and so far have been unsuccessful. The fact that you are going to be a father may stir feelings of disappointment, or even jealousy, in him.

ESSENTIAL

If the response of your parents or another close family member is somehow less than you expected, don't push it. Allow them the space to have their own personal reaction. They may need time to absorb the implications, just as you did.

Although this book is oriented toward first-time fathers, you may have already had a child. When you tell her the news, she may be beyond herself with excitement about the prospect of a new brother or sister. Still, amidst this happiness there may also be concern. She may be afraid the baby on the way will replace her in some way and that you will love the new baby more than her. Be sure to carve out some time for her to reassure her and make her feel special.

Early Workplace Strategies

Having a baby causes an earthquake in your personal and social life. But there is another area of your life that it greatly impacts as well: your job. How do you tell your employer? When is the best time to do that? These are questions every man must address sooner or later.

This, again, is another issue that is worth discussing with your partner. After the baby comes, one of you certainly needs to have a steady income. That will be the man in most cases, but your partner may need (or want) to resume her career after the baby is born. Both of you may need to be a little cagey in how you handle the news at work of her pregnancy and your impending fatherhood. This may or may not affect whether you make a public announcement on Facebook, for instance.

Assessing the Ground

In some companies, you may be able to walk right into your boss's office and blurt out, "Hey, I'm going to have a baby!" Your boss will stand up, shake your hand, and ask you how much time off you would like when the baby is born. Because, your boss will say, a job is only a job. But having a baby? Ah, nothing is more important than that.

If your company is like this (and you're not dreaming), you don't have a thing to worry about. Many companies, however, are not quite so enlightened. They may pay lip service to the whole fatherhood thing, but be far less supportive in reality. You will be the best judge of your company's work culture. When you become a father, you are no longer solely devoted to your job, and your employer may view you differently because of it. In this case, you may need to proceed cautiously.

Talk with Colleagues

If you are unsure, it makes sense to talk to a trusted friend at work who is also a parent to help you gauge how receptive management will be. Your friend can give you the lowdown on the best way to approach your boss or how to handle the situation with the company in general. He (or she) may tell you that your worries (if you have any) are groundless and that you can proceed with confidence. Or he may give you advice on how to avoid some of the pitfalls, if any, he encountered.

When seeking advice on this or any other pregnancy-related topic, you will usually find a natural ally in mothers. Because they have children themselves, they will be supportive of a man who wants to be an involved father. Chances are that if you work in a department or company with a lot of women, they may be more receptive to your pending fatherhood and the responsibilities it will entail than coworkers in a male-dominated environment.

Telling the Boss

It is may be best to put off telling your boss about your pending fatherhood until you have done some homework about your company's policies on parental leave and similar issues. It may also help to have an idea of what your plans are. For instance, how much time, if any, do you want to take off when the baby comes?

Again, this goes back to your work culture. Some jobs and companies will be open to a father taking some time off work after a baby comes. Others will be less keen on the idea. Reassuring your boss that even if you take some time off, it won't be long, and that you will make sure that your work gets covered so that the company will not miss a step while you are away, may put *his* worries to rest about the event.

Business Owner or Self-Employed

Many fathers-to-be run their own businesses. They are in the enviable position of not having to ask for time off from a boss; they are the boss and can just take the time as needed. Depending on the size of their business, though, they may not have employees who can simply step in for them while they take a week or so off.

Other fathers-to-be are self-employed and work at home. They have no staff at all. When they stop working, their entire business shuts down. With these men, as well as men who are employees in a company or organization, there will be pressure on them to get back to work as soon as possible after the baby is born. These and other work-related pressures and stresses will be considered in Chapter 9.

Learning that you are about to become a father can turn your world upside down. There are your own feelings to deal with, not to mention your partner's. You also have to deal with a whole bunch of other people: your families (hers and yours), doctors and medical specialists, friends, and coworkers to name a few. Then there are the issues of work and money. Nobody has all the answers in the beginning, but in the months to come be assured: you will figure them out.

CHAPTER 3

Riding the Pregnancy Roller Coaster

Being a father-to-be is like riding a roller coaster. You and your pregnant partner (especially your partner!) go up and down, and down and up, in a crazy and emotion-charged experience. The ride can be bumpy and unpredictable, particularly in the early months with the onset of morning sickness and the beginning of weight gain. Here is what to expect as you negotiate the curves.

The Stages of Pregnancy

Every man learns lots of new things in the process of becoming a father, including a few new words to add to his vocabulary. One of those words is "trimester." A trimester refers to one-third of a pregnancy, or roughly three months. Each trimester represents a stage in your child's development, and each carries its own rewards and challenges for both you and your partner.

As unique as every child is, as individual as every woman is, the process of having a baby is a fairly predictable process. Although there are endless small variations, the same things basically happen at the same time in every pregnancy. It is worthwhile to have a basic grasp of what happens during each of the three trimesters of a pregnancy because it will help you understand not only what you are going through at the moment, but also what lies ahead.

The First Trimester

The first trimester is approximately the first three months of the pregnancy, or the beginning of the ride. Your partner may still look like she has always looked in this period. Appearances can be deceiving, though. Inside her body, hormones and other chemicals are shooting off like firecrackers on the Fourth of July. Incredible metabolic changes are occurring although they may not be immediately apparent.

During the first few months, the child inside the womb grows with amazing rapidity. The umbilical cord is as thin as a human hair, yet the baby's tiny brain already has a skull around it. He has a sense of smell, and eyes and ears are formed. The fingers on his hands are segmenting. He can even suck his thumb by the end of the first trimester.

Generally, though, your partner will probably start to act a little differently than normal. Almost certainly she will become very, very tired. The ordinary chores of life—getting up in the morning to go to work, to name a big one—will be harder for her. In the early evening, after a day spent at work, she will likely be sacked out on the couch. This sudden fatigue she feels is brought on by the overtime her body is putting in on the pregnancy.

The changes you have heard so much about are beginning to occur. You do not have to wait for the baby to arrive to see changes in your partner or your relationship. They happen nearly at once, with the onset of pregnancy in the first trimester.

The Second, or Middle, Trimester

The second trimester is the middle three months of pregnancy, what you might call "the lull between storms." Although every woman is different, this is often the rosiest time of the pregnancy for both of you. Morning sickness and the extreme exhaustion have usually passed. She is beginning to show and is proud of it, but the baby is not so big yet that the pregnancy has become a huge burden, weighing her down physically and emotionally. You feel relieved because your partner is acting like herself again.

Many pregnant women report feeling on top of the world during this time, with energy surging through them. This renewed energy may allow the two of you to get reacquainted in the bedroom. The middle trimester is a good time to schedule a romantic weekend getaway and spend time together as a couple. Pretty soon your partner's nesting instincts will kick in, and after the baby is born you won't be able to go out together for a while, so now is the time.

QUOTE

"Go out on dates, sleep in, go to the movies, take walks, sip tea in bookstores," says Sarah McMoyler, a mother of two and nurse who teaches childbirth preparation classes. "Whatever you enjoy doing together, stock up on it. Newborns do one thing: inhale you whole. Invest in each other now; it will help hold you over during the early days of parenting."

One of the highlights of this period is that you get to feel the baby kick for the first time. Your partner lies on the bed or the couch, and you put your hand on her tummy. At first all you can hear is her stomach growling, but you wait…and be still…and wait some more…and then, boom! There it is. At that moment you would not trade your place in life with any man in the world.

The strong movements you feel the baby making at this stage happen because he has well-developed arms and legs. He is working them out. He has periods of activity and longer periods of calm in which he does not move at all. Able to react to sounds outside the womb, he can distinguish the voices of his mother and father by this time.

The Final Trimester

The last trimester is the home stretch, the final leg of this marathon race. Although each trimester roughly covers the same length of time, this one can feel like the longest of all. Your partner feels as big as a house, and everything she does—sitting, standing up, walking—is a monumental effort for her. Because of this, she is not always in the best of moods. Day by day she becomes more and more eager for the baby to be born, partly so the two of you can meet the newcomer but also so she can have her body to herself again.

The changes, as always, keep coming. Your partner may have left her job because she is simply too tired and uncomfortable to work anymore. She may be having what are called Braxton Hicks contractions, a sort of preparatory muscle movement that is readying her body to give birth. The baby, who weighs six to eight pounds (or more) and is about twenty inches long, sits right on her bladder forcing her to pee almost as often as you do when you're drinking beer.

ESSENTIAL

Pregnancy is a minefield for fathers-to-be. Even the most innocuous remark can drive your partner to tears or make her madder than hell at you. Be careful what you say. When in doubt, bite your tongue and say nothing. You will be better off in the long run. Always, always, always tell her you love her.

The closer you get to the due date, the more anxious you both become. Your partner visits the doctor once a week. She may not like to go out in public anymore because she's so uncomfortable. The two of you stay in closer touch with each other, just as your family and friends check in more often to see if there's anything they can do. But it's just a waiting game now.

Morning Sickness

Morning sickness usually takes place in the first three months of pregnancy. Some lucky women experience it only slightly or not at all, while others get raging cases. Morning sickness is actually a misnomer because it can occur throughout the day—morning, noon, and night.

No one knows exactly what causes it; it may be due to the wild and freaky hormonal changes occurring in a woman's body. It will not hurt the baby; in fact, it may help. Researchers have speculated that morning sickness may be nature's way of protecting the developing fetus from toxins that could harm it.

Morning sickness feels like a bad, bad hangover. Unfortunately, it's far worse than a hangover because it lasts for weeks and very little can be done to treat it. A woman in the grip of morning sickness feels like throwing up and sometimes does. She may have heartburn or a sour stomach, and ordinary cooking or food smells may seem ghastly and revolting to her. As a result, she may feel like eating only bland foods or maybe eating nothing at all.

ALERT

If your partner's morning sickness symptoms are extreme and a cause of worry, she should consult with her physician. This is a good rule of thumb for any concern that might arise during pregnancy, at any stage. Do not hesitate to seek medical advice.

This is a trying time for your partner. The first exhilarating days of pregnancy have rapidly turned sour. Luckily, there are some things you may be able to do to help. They include the following:

- Remind her to drink lots of fluids, particularly water, to prevent her from becoming dehydrated.
- Do some of the food shopping and preparation yourself, ensuring she gets the protein-rich, high-carbohydrate diet she needs.
- Stick with plain foods, such as rice or yogurt, and stay away from spicy and fatty dishes that may upset her stomach.

- Have her try to eat small meals throughout the day rather than a big meal at a single sitting. This is less likely to cause her problems.
- Tell her you love her and that you appreciate what she is already doing for the family.

Studies show that about 50 percent of all pregnant women experience morning sickness. Another way of looking at this statistic, however, is that 50 percent do not. Fortunately, morning sickness usually disappears after the first trimester, although some women can suffer nausea and vomiting throughout their pregnancies.

Cravings

Whenever you see fathers-to-be depicted in the movies or on television, two things invariably happen. One is that the man faints in the delivery room during childbirth (though this almost never happens in real life). The other thing you see occurs earlier in the pregnancy, when the woman develops some strange food craving and sends the man out in the middle of the night to get it for her.

Cravings are a normal and sometimes fun part of pregnancy. Also normal is the opposite of cravings: food aversion. Just as some pregnant women may develop cravings from time to time for pickles or peanut butter, they may also turn their nose up at food or beverages they formerly loved, such as a morning cup of java.

Studies show that up to 80 percent of all women experience food aversions of one kind or another during pregnancy. Cravings are even more common, with nine out of ten women saying they hungered for a certain food. The most popular food craving for pregnant women? Ice cream.

As with morning sickness, there are theories why women's bodies instinctively react in this manner. Those raging hormones, as always, lie at the root of it, but it may be that the reason a woman craves certain foods is that her body needs what those foods are supplying her with. Conversely, she may feel less than enamored by certain previously indulged-in items such as coffee or alcohol.

So what's a man to do if his pregnant partner develops a sudden taste for prestirred mixed-berry yogurt at four in the morning? The answer to that one is simple. He throws on his clothes, grabs the car keys, and goes to get it. Your partner will consider you a hero, and the two of you can sit in bed and eat berry yogurt together while watching the sunrise.

Her Changing Body

If most of the attention during pregnancy seems to be focused on the woman, it is because that is where it rightly belongs. In so many other areas of a man's life he can claim to be the top dog, the leader of the pack. But not in this one. The woman is the lead player, and if you have any doubts about that all you have to do is look at her body, which is beginning to look a little, well, plump.

The first, last, and foremost rule in dealing with your partner during this time is never—never!—make jokes about her body. If she wants to make jokes about it, fine. If she wants to poke fun at herself, fine. But you? *Never.*

You really do want to boost your partner's spirits. She needs all the support she can get because her body is putting her through the wringer. It seems to be changing on a daily, even hourly basis, in a thousand weird and wacky ways. Here are a few of the things that are happening to her:

- Constipation and hemorrhoids
- Back pain and sciatica
- Tender, sore, and enlarged breasts
- Aches and pains of all sorts
- Super-sensitive nipples
- Splotchy, flaky, or itchy skin
- Leg and stomach cramps
- Breathlessness

Your partner has a new, developing shape that she is still learning to live with. Her center of balance is shifting, making her clumsier at times. She also may be more forgetful than usual, more distracted and absent-minded. Be gentle and patient. After all, she is building your baby.

Sympathy Pains

Some men experience physical sensations when their partner is pregnant. These are commonly known as "sympathy pains." Another term for it is the couvade syndrome. "Couvade" is a French word that means "to hatch," so another way to explain this is that the rooster feels a little bit of what the hen is going through.

Physical Signs

The most common of these feelings are stomach pains and discomfort. Many men also say they have food cravings, much like their pregnant partner, and experience some gain weight. These symptoms tend to crop up early in the pregnancy, in the third month or so, and they vanish just as mysteriously as they arrived after the baby is born.

FACT

One out of four fathers-to-be experience gastrointestinal discomfort during their partner's pregnancy. Less common aches and pains are headaches, itching, nose bleeds, and toothaches. In some cultures, when a man complains of a toothache, his dentist is taught to ask him if his partner is pregnant.

No one knows exactly why this occurs. These feelings are not purely in a guy's head, as some might think. They are actual physical sensations. Some speculate that the couvade is another way in which the man tries to protect his partner. Since there is little he can do to ease her discomfort, his brain tries to take on some of these pains and thus relieve her.

Another theory is that male hormones cause these symptoms. Men have hormones just as women do, just in smaller doses. One recent study suggests that a man's hormones change to correspond with the hormonal changes in his pregnant partner's body. This may explain why men who could not have cared less about kids for most of their adult lives begin to show more interest in babies in the last months of their partner's pregnancy.

No Sympathy for Your Sympathy Pains

One thing is certain about your sympathy pains: don't expect much sympathy for them. No matter what happened with your body, you know, along with everyone else, that this is nothing compared to what your partner is going through.

Some people say that sympathy pains are nothing more than the man's attempt to get people to pay attention to him. The man is jealous, in this view, that all the focus in his relationship has shifted to his partner, and he is feeling left out. He wants people to recognize that he is the father and that he's part of this program, too. In fact, sympathy pains bring up a larger issue that has nothing to do with the pains themselves but everything to do with a man's role during his partner's pregnancy. Chapter 6 covers some of the myriad worries you may experience.

If you're having sympathy pains, do you talk about them with your partner? Most men might mention them in a casual conversation over the breakfast table or in bed. It's no big deal. Your partner may appreciate the fact that you're suffering a little along with her, and she may see it as another sign that you're fully involved with the pregnancy and coming to grips mentally with this huge event in your lives.

A Volatile Issue: Her Weight

Every man knows how sensitive the issue of weight is to a woman. It's like a hair-trigger explosive: touch it in the wrong way—or even touch it at all—and it is going to explode in your face. Most smart men never venture within miles of it. Those who do, do so only at extreme risk.

When women become pregnant, the issue of weight becomes even more sensitive of a topic. Suddenly they can no longer fit into their jeans. In fact, none of their clothes fit. Sometimes even their feet grow in size so their shoes don't fit either. They look in the mirror and see somebody they hardly recognize.

Some women cannot stand the way they look during pregnancy. It is so contrary to their normal body image that they think they look fat and ugly. The early months may be the hardest for them because they're not really showing and yet they're still putting on pounds. People who do not know they're pregnant may just think they're gaining weight, and this adds to their misery. These feelings lighten during the middle trimester, when the pregnant woman clearly begins to show.

Physicians recommend that women gain twenty-five to thirty-five pounds during pregnancy, but it is quite common for women to gain as many as fifty pounds or more in the months before giving birth. They will shed most of these pounds once the baby is born, although the more weight a woman gains, the harder it will be for her to return to her prepregnancy self.

All of this puts the man in a sizable bind. He wants his partner to gain weight; it is what she is supposed to be doing. Her weight gain means that the baby is growing and getting bigger and stronger, all of which is good. But what should he do, if anything, if his partner keeps getting bigger…and bigger…and bigger?

Take Charge of Healthy Eating

One approach is to take charge of doing the food shopping and meal preparation (if you haven't already), so that you know your partner is getting the right kinds of food. Fix meals full of green, leafy vegetables bursting with folic acid; protein-rich meat, chicken, and fish; and other healthy options. Without needing to say one word about her weight, you can still be helping her in this regard.

ALERT

Some pregnant women have a different dilemma: not gaining enough weight. This is nothing to be alarmed about early in the pregnancy, but it should be monitored because it can affect the baby's growth later on. Encouraging your partner to eat several small nutrition-packed meals a day may help her add pounds.

Another way to help is with meals outside the home. Does she eat junk food? Do you? Taking a little break from the greasy, high-fat meals at fast-food places is not much of a sacrifice to make.

Be fair. You can't expect her to eat healthy foods while you down fries and donuts in front of her. The same holds true for smoking and drinking. Don't smoke in her presence, and lower your alcohol intake so she won't be as tempted.

Be Complimentary

Whatever you think of your partner's growing size, you can be certain that criticizing her isn't a good approach. You would like her to gain enough weight so that she and the baby are healthy, but not so many pounds she has a hard time losing the weight after she gives birth. This may not seem like a lot to ask, but putting her down or making fun of her will surely not help her. She will only resent you for your lack of sympathy, and it may hurt your relationship.

Here's a better tactic: flood her with kindness. Tell her she looks beautiful, and keep telling her that for the next nine months and beyond, even if you secretly are thinking something else. It will make her feel better, and the burden she's carrying will seem a little lighter.

Get into It!

Women gain weight when they're pregnant, to be sure. That's what they're supposed to do. Instead of experiencing it as a negative, however, try seeing it in a different way. Many women look sexy wearing the extra pounds that come with pregnancy. Ever see any pictures of Heidi Klum decked out in a form-fitting runway dress when she was five or six months pregnant? Not bad, not bad at all.

It is not just Hollywood stars who "glow" during this time. Pregnancy can add vitality to a woman's appearance and curves to her shape that are a real turn-on.

Women's breasts go through a notable change: they get bigger. Although the woman's nipples may become overly sensitive, for men, larger and fuller breasts do not generally pose a problem. Even before the baby comes, some women produce milk from their breasts. The taste of breast milk is sweet, and there is no reason why a man cannot enjoy this taste too.

The Emotional Roller Coaster

The physical changes that your partner is experiencing may be accompanied by sudden and abrupt mood swings that can only be compared to riding a roller coaster. One minute she is on a hormone-induced high, feeling free as a bird and as good as she has ever felt in her entire life. Five minutes later, tears are pouring down her face because she cannot button the top button on her jeans. A little while after that, she feels irritable or defensive and snaps at you for some remark you made that she perceived to be offensive.

QUOTE

Katie Lynn, mother of two, tells all new fathers and fathers-to-be not to take their partner's mood swings personally. "It's really not about you," she says to men. "Try as best you can to listen and validate what she's going through because chances are she is feeling crazy enough as it is without hearing an argument from you."

While this may appear to you to be irrational behavior, put yourself in her shoes. A tiny, demanding, hungry little human being is growing inside her. In many respects, this fetal beast has taken over her body. If this were happening to you, you probably would not be in the cheeriest of moods either.

Be Even and Steady

When your loving and long-suffering partner gets a little grumpy, it is understandable if you become a little grumpy yourself. You're not Gandhi, after all. You have emotions just like she does, and you're entitled to show them.

All couples argue, pregnant or not. There is no way to avoid that. Just realize that your partner's emotional state may be more ragged and unpredictable than normal. A better approach for you, if you can manage it, is to be steady as you go. You can help her by being the rock against which her emotional waves can crash.

Hold Her Hand

One thing you should realize is that the changing nature of your partner's moods may upset her too. Her body, she has found, is no longer completely under her control, and now her emotions are going crazy on her as well. It may be scary to her and make her think that her entire life is out of balance.

If pregnancy is like a roller-coaster ride, what would you do to comfort your partner if she felt genuinely scared on an actual roller-coaster ride? What if she began to cry uncontrollably or scream because she feared that the car you were riding in was going to tip over or break? You almost certainly would reach over and touch her hand to reassure her. This is also something you can do for your partner when she is upset or anxious or fearful about her pregnancy.

ESSENTIAL

Another reason why many pregnant women feel miserable is the clothes they must wear. Nice-looking maternity clothes are expensive. Some mothers-to-be only have a couple of outfits that they feel comfortable and look good in and, consequently, they wear them to death. Kind words go a long way.

Hold your partner's hand. Caress her hand or forehead. Put your arm around her and embrace her. Rub her feet. Cuddle her in a nonsexual way in bed. Through all these ways and more you can show your partner that you care about her and understand what she's going through.

Remember, This Too Shall Pass

The nine to ten months of pregnancy may feel like an eternity at times, but they actually pass fairly quickly, especially when you consider the years and years you are going to spend raising your child. It is good to remember throughout pregnancy—and, for that matter, when you're a parent—that this too shall pass. Nothing lasts forever.

Your partner's morning sickness is going to pass. She is going to move on from the first trimester of pregnancy into the middle and later stages. She is going to gain weight and, after the baby comes, she will lose weight. Once the baby arrives, the concerns she had while she was pregnant will be replaced by other concerns that have to do with raising a child—concerns that you, as the child's father, will certainly share.

All this is the way it is supposed to be, and the way it has always been. It is impossible to change any of it, and why would you want to? It may sound trite, but it is true: while you are on this wild roller coaster of a ride, try to enjoy each moment as much as possible.

Look at how much you've learned about pregnancy already—the stages that are involved, how quickly (and amazingly) your baby is developing, your partner's changing body, and how this can affect her moods. The great thing is that the more knowledge you have, the less anxious you feel, and the more enjoyable the whole experience becomes. This rule also applies to the process of learning how to be a birth coach and the medical aspects of the pregnancy.

CHAPTER 4

Doctors and Medical Tests

Having a baby is a physical and emotional experience. It is also a medical one. Physicians, nurses, nurse-midwives, healthcare specialists, and others will help you and your partner deliver your baby. Here are some tips on how to deal with what can be an intimidating world for men.

The Obstetrician

Next to you and the baby, your partner's obstetrician is the most important person in her life. Family physicians also provide prenatal care, but this is less common today. No matter what his or her exact title is, the physician is the person who oversees and coordinates your partner's care.

Depending on your medical plan, this doctor may not, however, actually deliver your baby. The physicians at your hospital may work on a rotating basis. In this system, your partner's doctor will be the attending physician, and deliver your baby, only if he or she is on duty the night you come in to have your baby. If not, you will get the physician who happens to be on duty that night. At some hospitals, the doctor your partner has seen throughout the pregnancy does indeed commit to seeing her all the way through to birth.

FACT

Obstetricians provide most of the prenatal care in America today. Surveys show that about 80 percent of all pregnant women receive care from an obstetrician. Midwives provide care to 13 percent of pregnant women, while family physicians deliver care to the other 7 percent.

The doctor can answer medical questions about pregnancy or refer you to a specialist if you have questions he or she cannot answer. But a good doctor has more than just medical skills and know-how; a good doctor functions as a reassuring figure to the nervous mom-to-be, who will come to count on the physician as the person who has been down this road many times before and can show her the way.

Your Relationship with Her Doctor

In the not-so-distant past, fathers were seen as unwelcome intruders in a hospital or doctor's office. While the attitudes of the medical profession have changed considerably, you still may feel like an unnecessary and perhaps unwanted person. You may be treated with coolness or disdain. You may be patronized and not taken seriously. When speaking, the doctor may look only at your partner, not at you, even if you were the one who asked the question.

Not every medical professional acts like this. Many see the father as a truly important person, not just someone who gets in the way. They talk to both the man and the woman, answer their questions directly, and treat them as equals who are sharing this adventure together.

Don't act like a potted plant if the doctor treats you coolly or ignores you. Speak up and ask questions. Make direct eye contact and appear interested and involved. If necessary, tell the doctor directly that you wish to be included.

Being There

Given that many fathers-to-be feel like the proverbial fifth wheel when they visit the doctor with their pregnant partners, it is understandable that some choose not to go at all. The partners of these guys go solo (or with mother or sister or girlfriend), and the men find out what they need to know when the woman gets home. It is also likely that this father-to-be will be at work and unable to take the time off.

Even the most involved father-to-be need not attend every prenatal checkup, but every man should go to at least one early in the pregnancy (in addition to the ultrasound). That gives you a chance to meet your partner's doctor, the person who will be overseeing her care throughout the pregnancy and who may end up delivering your baby. This also gives you the opportunity to ask questions and get answers directly from a medical expert.

Of course, your partner may need you to go to more than just one or two visits, at which point you are going to have to rearrange your schedule and be there. You will certainly want to be on hand for the ultrasound exams and the amniocentesis, if one is called for.

Prenatal Doctor Visits

Typically, a pregnant woman pays one or two visits to the doctor in her first trimester. In the middle trimester, the frequency of her visits increases to about once a month. Entering the final trimester, trips to the doctor become biweekly affairs until, at about the thirty-six-week mark, she sees the doctor once a week. Depending on your partner's medical history and her specific health issues, a doctor may want to see her more often.

One of the coolest prenatal visits for dads occurs at about twelve weeks, when you hear the baby's heartbeat for the first time. The doctor lubricates your partner's tummy with some slippery goop, and then runs a handheld ultrasound instrument—known as an ultrasound Doppler—over the lubricated area. The Doppler picks up and amplifies the sound coming from inside the womb. The sound of your child's beating heart is sure to give you a smile, a laugh, or even a chill.

FACT

After three months, the baby is twenty-seven to thirty-one millimeters long, about twice the size of your thumbnail. Her heart, which has been beating for a while, is now strong enough that instruments can pick up the sound. While the fetal heart pumps only one-fifth the blood of an adult heart, it has already developed valves and four chambers.

Hearing the heartbeat is another of those signposts along the pregnancy road that is particularly meaningful to Dad. The idea of having a baby is still pretty abstract to him up to this point. Hearing that little thumper makes it a lot more real. The realization steadily dawns that an actual, honest-to-goodness human being is inside there.

Monitoring Progress

A woman undergoes a battery of tests throughout her pregnancy. She is poked at and pricked with needles. Every time she walks into a doctor's office she is asked for a urine sample and has to pee in a cup. Similarly, her weight is checked religiously and her blood pressure is taken repeatedly. You may (or may not) be intimidated when you see your partner's doctors and nurses, but by the time her pregnancy is over they will feel like old friends to her.

The tests performed on your partner are designed to monitor her health, the condition of the developing fetus, and the possible development of any birth defects. Here are several of the more common tests that are customarily administered at the first prenatal visit:

- Blood tests check for iron deficiency (anemia), blood type, and hormonal levels.
- Urinalysis measures sugar or glucose levels, white blood cells, and bacteria.
- Blood screens gauge immunity to rubella and other diseases.
- Other tests determine if syphilis, gonorrhea, hepatitis B, chlamydia, or HIV are present.
- Genetic tests check for sickle cell anemia, Tay-Sachs, and other possible genetic diseases.
- Pap smear is taken to detect cervical cancer.
- Triple screen or expanded alpha-fetoprotein blood test checks for possible birth defects (second trimester).
- Glucose screening tests for gestational diabetes (also usually in second trimester)

Medical test results are often loaded down with numbers that mean something to physicians but almost nothing to lay people. You and your partner may have questions after these tests are done, especially if the results are not what you expected. This is definitely a good time to fly the family colors and go with your partner to her doctor. Writing down your questions ahead of time will help you remember everything you want to ask in the sometimes rushed, high-pressure environment of a doctor's office.

Ultrasound Exams

Going to the ultrasound exam is one of the early highlights of pregnancy. It's the first time you will see your baby (well, sort of). Two ultrasounds may be conducted early in pregnancy—the first is usually done before twelve weeks and the second between eighteen and twenty-two weeks. Both visits are a kick in the pants that you absolutely must not miss.

Ultrasound technology, known as sonography, represents a major step forward in obstetrics. It uses sound waves that are inaudible to the human ear to create a visual image of the baby's environment inside the womb—not an HDTV-quality image, mind you, but an image nonetheless. An ultrasound or sonogram is not an X-ray and is regarded as completely safe. Even so, it is done only when medically necessary.

What Ultrasound Does

An ultrasound exam provides lots of vital information. It can provide accurate information about how far along your partner is in the pregnancy and nail down the baby's due date. It can help doctors look for abnormalities in the fetus and note how it is developing. The ultrasound also provides a wealth of technical information, such as the amount of amniotic fluid in the amniotic sac, what kind of shape the placenta is in (and where it is), and other hard facts.

An ultrasound exam may carry a surprise or two as well. You may learn that you have not one but two munchkins swimming around in there. A sonographer may also be able to ascertain whether your child is a boy or a girl, if you care to know.

What You Can Expect

Since an ultrasound is such a big moment in the life of pregnant couples, sonographers are quite comfortable with having men around. In some ways an ultrasound resembles a good television show. Both you and your partner will have your eyes glued to the monitor, trying to detect every possible detail about your child. Meanwhile, the sonographer serves as your host and guide, telling you exactly what you are looking at as she records the information she needs to know.

Your partner lies on her back on a table, exposing her stomach. The sonographer rubs some lubricating goo on her skin and places a device on her tummy that directs sound waves at her uterus and fetus. The echoes created by these sound waves produce the visual images you see on the monitor.

But don't expect to see too much. Reading the monitor is like trying to read a traffic sign fifty yards away in the middle of a blizzard. Still, it's an exciting experience, like being given the chance to peer into this secret world. With the sonographer's assistance, you will be able to pinpoint features on your child—his hands and arms, his legs and feet, his head. When the ten- to fifteen-minute visit is over, you get a picture of your kid that you can show your friends and family and tape to the front of your refrigerator at home.

Boy or Girl?

Besides the fact that the ultrasound gives couples the chance to see their baby for the first time, it is an important event in the life of a couple for another reason. This is often when you learn your child's gender. Although parents-to-be can learn whether the baby is a boy or a girl at the first ultrasound (before the twelve-week mark), this revelation generally occurs during the second visit, at roughly the twenty-week point in the pregnancy. The fetus is larger, and his or her gender is easier to identify (though it is not always possible to tell for certain).

ALERT

Although the technology continues to improve and the pictures they rely on are becoming clearer, sonographers have been known to make mistakes in guessing a child's gender. Because their determinations are based on visual evidence, they are not 100 percent accurate. Most of the time, though, sonographers are right on the money.

You and your partner must decide. Do you want to know the gender? As with so many things having to do with pregnancy, there is no right or wrong decision. Whatever works for the two of you is the right decision.

Some couples prefer not to know. They enjoy the guessing game and the suspense leading up to the big moment when the baby is finally born. If you do not want to know your child's gender, be sure to tell your doctor and the people at the ultrasound exams. You do not want them to spill the beans accidentally.

Other couples choose not to wait until after the baby is born to find out; they want to know as soon as they can. There are some practical advantages to this approach. Knowing the baby's gender may make it easier to decide on nursery decorations or what kind of clothes to buy. Also, there is only one name to choose.

The Moment You Learn the News

Just as when your partner told you she was pregnant you were in a reactive position, you will be reacting again when you learn the gender of your child. Unlike when you heard about the pregnancy for the first time, however, this information is not news that your partner necessarily has first. She does not know the child's gender; she is as out of the loop as you are. The one with the information is the sonographer. This is the person who will tell you whether you have a boy or girl.

Your partner is lying on her back with her head turned to look at the monitor while the sonographer moves the ultrasound device around her belly. This is not a comfortable position for her, nor a relaxed moment. She is happy, excited, anxious, nervous, fearful, and curious all at the same time.

One reason for her anxiety is you. Whether she says so or not, she is searching your face for clues about how you feel. The sonographer has just told you the news—boy or girl—and your partner, in her discomfort on the table, is looking to you for your reaction. Once again, what you do and say in this moment matters—a lot.

The Choices You Make

Each man will have his own reaction when he learns the gender of his child. Although the geneticists point out that the creation of a boy or a girl is a random act, merely a matter of the victorious sperm's chromosomal makeup, everyone knows that it is much more than that. It is big, and the issues it engenders are complex.

Many fathers-to-be want to have a son. Though they may not be willing to admit it, they feel that having a son signifies virility. They may believe that people will consider them more masculine if they have a son. They may also feel like they will have more in common with a boy than a girl.

FACT

A child's gender is determined at the instant of creation. Human beings have twenty-three pairs, or sets, of chromosomes. The twenty-third set is known as the sex chromosomes. In females, the sex chromosomes are XX, while in males, they are XY. The unfertilized egg carries only X, or female, chromosomes. If the egg is fertilized by a sperm carrying only the X chromosome, the fetus gets an X from the sperm and an X from the egg—making it XX, or female. If the sperm that fertilizes the egg carries Y, the fetus gets the Y from the sperm and an X from the egg—making it XY, or male.

A smaller proportion of men want a daughter. For one reason or another, they're not sure about boys. For them, a boy represents a potential threat to their status. With Mom and daughter around, they will be the man in the family, and they like that.

Sonographers report that some men sulk after hearing the news of their child's gender. They suddenly lose interest in what is going on. Their attention strays. They pick up a magazine and begin leafing through the pages or even stand up and leave the room.

If your first reaction is disappointment or ambivalence, remember that love is not static. Your feelings are only beginning, and they will grow and deepen over time—no matter what the gender of your child. Remember that woman lying on the table gazing up at you for your reaction? She needs you—it's as simple as that. Reach over and hold her hand.

Surprise! It's Twins!

The other big piece of news you could learn at the ultrasound is that you're having twins. Based on some of the symptoms your partner has been experiencing, her doctor may have suspected as much. The sonogram may have been ordered to confirm a preliminary diagnosis. An ultrasound will be able to detect the presence of twins in almost every case.

Carrying twins (or triplets or other multiples) is considered a "high-risk" pregnancy. This term is nothing to get frightened about—women deliver twins safely all the time. In fact, nearly one out of every forty-one couples has twins these days. But the medical issues involved in carrying and delivering twins are more complicated than if you're just having one. You and your partner need to have a sit-down talk with your obstetrician to get straight on how you're going to proceed from here.

As the prospective father of twins, you may have greater responsibilities during your partner's pregnancy than other fathers-to-be. Your partner is, in effect, doing double duty, and you may need to pitch in extra to help her out. Here are some things to be aware of:

- Your partner will need to see the doctor more often, which may require you to go to more visits.

- Because low birth weight can be a problem for some twins, her diet is crucial, which may mean you need to shop for food and cook more.
- She will need a ton of rest, so you'll need to pitch in with more of the housework and other duties.
- Her doctor may recommend that she stop working after only six or seven months, which means that you may need to get your financial house in order sooner than other fathers-to-be.
- Because twins typically arrive weeks earlier than a standard pregnancy, you and your spouse should take childbirth classes in the second trimester and make sure you know the signs of early labor.

The parents of twins sometimes have an intense emotional reaction when they learn the news that they are going to have two babies at once. Many are in shock at first. Slowly this shock may turn into worry or disappointment or even fear. Such feelings are normal, and there is no reason to feel guilty about having them.

Amniocentesis

The ultrasound is a tool used by physicians to diagnose the status of the growing child and check in on how she is faring inside the womb. Two other commonly used diagnostic tools are chorionic villus sampling, or CVS, and amniocentesis, although many couples never have either of these tests done. Both tests have a degree of risk attached, and they are only performed when there are clear benefits to be gained.

CVS is done when there is a family history of genetic disease or if there are other medical indicators that might suggest a need for the test. It is performed early in the pregnancy, between ten and twelve weeks. Usually done in a hospital, CVS is a surgical procedure in which a small sample is taken from the placenta. Chromosomal analysis of this tissue can detect the presence of Down syndrome, many forms of cystic fibrosis, and other genetic disorders.

Amniocentesis is recommended for pregnant women aged thirty-five or older—what the medical profession describes as "advanced maternal age." Younger women normally do not need to consider this procedure. Even some women thirty-five and older choose not to have it. It is an optional procedure that couples may decline if they wish.

The primary purpose of an "amnio," as it is called, is to see if the fetus has Down syndrome, which occurs most frequently in women of advanced maternal age. But it is also used to test for spina bifida and other chromosomal defects as well. An amnio usually takes place in the second trimester, between the sixteenth and eighteenth weeks, and it can be done in the same office where your partner has her ultrasound. The procedure is often done in conjunction with the second ultrasound visit.

ESSENTIAL

Here, again, is where the importance of talking comes in. Talk with your partner. Sit in on her discussions with her obstetrician about these procedures. Perhaps talk with another couple who has faced a similar decision and gone ahead with an amnio. The more information you have, the better you will feel about the decision you ultimately make.

In an amniocentesis, your partner lies on her back just as she did during the ultrasound. Using the sonograph as a guide, a physician inserts a hollow needle into her stomach though the wall of the abdomen. Amniotic fluids are withdrawn from the womb through the needle. It takes about a week to get the results of the laboratory analysis of the cells in the fluid. An amnio will also establish for certain the gender of your child (though it is never done just for this purpose).

One reason that both CVS and amniocentesis are serious medical procedures is that each carries a small risk of miscarriage. You and your partner must weigh this risk against the benefits to be obtained from either procedure. Your doctor can help lay out the clinical facts, but ultimately, like so many other issues having to do with your child, the two of you will make a decision based on your values and what you feel is the right thing to do.

Miscarriage

Miscarriage is the loss of a child during pregnancy. It can occur for a variety of reasons, some known and some unknown. When it occurs, a miscarriage can be an emotionally devastating event for both parents.

The risk of miscarriage is highest in the first trimester. Most miscarriages occur within the first twelve weeks of pregnancy, although they can and do occur later on. In one study, miscarriages occurred in 15 percent of all reported pregnancies. After suffering a miscarriage, however, nearly nine in ten women have a healthy pregnancy the next time.

Living with the Threat

Because of worry about the possibility of miscarriage, many couples do not immediately tell other people that they are pregnant. They wait until after three months have passed, the period considered most likely for a miscarriage, before breaking the news. Some older couples wait even longer, until after reviewing the amniocentesis results at roughly the twenty-week mark. When that goes well and everything is fine with the baby, they let their families and friends in on the secret.

ALERT

There are several warning signs of potential miscarriage, such as heavy bleeding and severe cramps. If your partner reports these symptoms, you should act immediately. Call your doctor or medical practitioner and, if necessary, take her to the emergency room.

Your partner may feel the threat of miscarriage more acutely than you do. On top of the many physical discomforts she experiences early in pregnancy, she may worry that she will do something that will cause her to lose her child. This is another thing to keep in mind as her emotions swing up and down during this vulnerable time.

Sex and Miscarriage

Early miscarriage remains shrouded in mystery. No one knows exactly what causes it in many cases. A healthy woman who is doing everything right can still lose a child.

One thing a man may wonder about is sexual intercourse. Can it harm the baby or cause a miscarriage? In a normal pregnancy, the answer is no. You should talk to the doctor if your partner's pregnancy is considered high-risk or if she has a history of miscarriage.

Another thing a man thinks about is how much weight his partner can safely pick up and carry when she's pregnant. She can continue to do normal household activities, such as carrying light bags of groceries and carefully picking up young children. These will not normally cause harm. Moving large furniture or heavy objects, however, should be your job.

The Emotional Toll

Losing a child, even a child who is still in the womb, can take a heavy emotional toll on the parents. It seems so unfair, so random. So many other couples have babies. why can't we have one? Why did it have to happen to us?

A woman may blame herself. She may feel intense guilt over the loss, as if she was responsible for it. Where there was once a child inside her, now there is only emptiness. She may become depressed. You will almost certainly experience similar feelings of sadness and disappointment.

As sad as a miscarriage is, couples can and do recover from it and go on to have healthy babies. Some mothers may even express a sense of relief at a miscarriage because they inwardly suspected something was wrong with the pregnancy. Nature took its course, for whatever reason, and they are willing to accept it and move on with their lives.

Trying Again

It is probably going to take some time before you are both ready to move on and try again. You will certainly need to do plenty of talking. And it may be valuable for both you and your partner to talk to other parents who have experienced a loss of this kind. Your local hospital may sponsor a support group for parents who have suffered a miscarriage.

Go with your partner to at least one or two of these sessions. You may be surprised at who you meet there. You may find other men there who have lost children and are grieving about it. They will tell the story of what happened to them, and then you can tell your story. Through this process, you will probably discover feelings of grief and hurt that you did not know were there.

Many, many couples become pregnant again and have a child after a miscarriage. If there were known medical reasons that caused the event, however, you may need to resolve those issues before trying again. Some doctors recommend waiting six months or so for your partner's body to recover. No one but you and your partner, though, can decide when you are ready to give it another go. Before moving on, it is worthwhile to take some time to absorb the loss and let the wounds heal.

Pregnancy is a journey. Some journeys, sadly, do not end the way you want them to. But with today's prenatal medicine, the high level of professionalism and expertise among doctors, nurses, health-care specialists and staff, and the sophisticated testing that is done on mothers and babies in the womb, you can be confident that you are going to receive lots and lots of help along the way. The knowledge you are gaining about this whole process will help you as well.

CHAPTER 5

Your Suddenly Expanding Family

When you learn your partner is pregnant, you obviously expect to welcome, at some point, a new person into your family. Keep in mind, though, that a baby widens your social circle beyond just you and your partner. Suddenly a whole bunch of people—parents, parents-in-law, aunts- and uncles-to-be, other relatives, her close friends—are an intimate part of your life.

Your Shifting Social World

Having a child is the greatest thing that can happen to a man, but it still causes worry. One of the potential trouble spots (or so a father-to-be thinks) is in the social arena, particularly as it relates to his partner. Many men consider their partner as their best friend. She provides their deepest emotional support. She is the social leader of the family, inviting friends over for dinner and arranging get-togethers. How will that change when the baby comes?

Your Partner

If your partner is pregnant you have almost certainly noticed subtle shifts beginning to take place in your social world. Some of these shifts may not be subtle at all. Your partner may be utterly exhausted when she gets home from work and fast asleep on the couch by eight o'clock. She may be too tired to go out on the weekends.

ESSENTIAL

If you're feeling cut off from your partner's whirl in the pregnancy social circle, there is a simple fix. Join it. Accompany her on her visits to the doctor. Take the childbirth classes. Talk to her about baby names. Spend an afternoon with her shopping for baby clothes or gear. It won't kill you, and you may even enjoy it.

With your partner sacking out early most nights, you have to do more chores around the house, which puts a dent in your free time. Not only that, you're more tired. When you finally do get a chance to go out with the guys, you feel guilty because you're out enjoying yourself while your partner is stuck at home. If you cut the night short, you'll feel bad because, in your mind, your friends think you're already turning into a dud even before the baby is born.

It is important to realize that your social life does not end when you have a baby; all it does is change. In many ways, it changes for the better, but these changes can be unsettling at first.

Your Friends

One of the things that happens when your partner becomes pregnant is that your social life becomes far less spontaneous. In the old days, your friends might have called you up at the last minute to go to a movie or hear some music. If it sounded like fun, you went along without thinking twice about it. That is much less likely to happen nowadays.

Many of your guy friends may be in their twenties or thirties. They may be single and have never had kids. How will they react when Junior arrives and you're knee-deep in diapers?

For obvious reasons, your childless friends are going to have a harder time adjusting to your new reality. They're still able to go to a ballgame or out to dinner whenever they feel like it. After you turn down their invitations to go out a couple of times in a row, they may mentally stick you in the "Married with Children" column and stop calling altogether. And you may find it harder to find the time to call them.

It is inevitable that you will see less and less of your friends who don't have children than you did before. What happens is that they will be slowly replaced with a different sort of animal: couples with small children like your own. Along with your expanding extended family, these people steadily become fixtures in your new social world.

Her Family

One of the biggest changes that occurs in your social world when your partner becomes pregnant is that her relatives and friends become more involved in your family life than ever before. Conversely, you become more involved with them. Because they are calling the house more often, you talk on the phone more with them. Because they are dropping by to see your partner more often, you tend to have more occasions to see them as well.

No matter how many years you have been married or in a relationship with the mother-to-be, or how well you think you know your in-laws, with a baby on the way you are going to have an opportunity get to know them much, much better.

Your Mother-in-Law

Like the father who faints on the delivery room floor during childbirth, the mother-in-law is one of the staples of television and movie comedies. She is often depicted as a loud, pushy, overbearing, domineering woman who bosses everyone around, including the mother- and father-to-be. Like the fainting dad, this caricature usually bears little relation to reality.

Whatever your mother-in-law's personality, she does have one thing that you and your partner do not yet possess: actual, real-life baby experience. She did it. In fact, she birthed and raised the girl who grew up to be the woman you fell in love with and chose to make the mother of your child. If for no other reason than that, you need to listen to what your mother-in-law says with an open mind.

Make no mistake. Your mother-in-law—along with your own mother and probably every other person you know in the world—will be giving you advice. You will receive advice on everything under the sun having to do with babies because, well, that is what happens when you are about to become a parent. People give you advice, whether you ask for it or not.

There are 60 to 70 million grandparents in the United States. About one in ten grandparents provide child care for their grandchildren on a regular basis. The most common activities that grandparents and grandchildren do together are eating, watching television, spending the night, shopping, and exercise or sports.

Depending on their personalities, your mother-in-law and mother will likely be leaders in the advice sweepstakes. So be prepared. Some of what they say will be hard to hear. Some of it will sound like criticism. But every now and then, their seasoned words will hit the bull's-eye right smack dab in the middle and you will be honestly and deeply grateful for their advice.

Your Father-in-Law

In television sitcoms and movies, the father-in-law is also a comic figure. But unlike her, the father-in-law is usually the quiet type, a man who has gotten used to being pushed around over the years and has learned to live with it. Again, this caricature may or may not have anything to do with your reality. Chances are good that both your father-in-law and father did not participate as actively as you are in their partner's pregnancy or the birth of their children.

QUESTION

What if I don't get along with an in-law?
Don't sweat it. The pregnancy has improved your position in the family hierarchy. The in-laws will all want to have some relationship with the baby, and they will want to be on good terms with the baby's father, too.

Still, that doesn't mean they won't offer advice. They know a thing or two about being a parent, and they will likely share it with you at some point. Don't disregard their perspectives. One thing they may confess to you is how lucky they think you are to participate in your child's birth, something they may not have done or, if they did, not as much as they would have liked.

Your Family

The imminent arrival of a newborn can bring families and friends together. But it can also sometimes cause friction. If one family—say, your partner's—moves strongly into the picture, it may cause your family to withdraw or become resentful of how much influence the other side has. You need to learn how to balance the various concerns of family members.

This is a fact of life when you have a baby. Before the pregnancy it was just you and your partner. Now that you are about to become a threesome, your extended family will be getting much more involved in your lives. Usually this is a good thing, but sometimes there are issues to deal with because of it.

Your Mother

When a woman becomes pregnant, she almost inevitably draws closer to her mother, who, having gone through all of this before, is a reassuring and comforting figure. Even if the two live 3,000 miles apart, they find ways to connect. Maybe they e-mail or connect on Facebook, or maybe they choose to talk more on the phone. The mother comes to visit, and the daughter returns the favor and visits her. If her mother lives close by, the two often become like girlfriends, shopping for baby clothes, checking out baby gear, and so forth.

It is simply not the same experience for fathers-to-be and their mothers. In fact, what may happen is that the man becomes closer to his partner's mother because he starts seeing her more frequently than he did before, leaving his own mother feeling left out.

Again, this scenario may never unfold. Because you are going to be a parent, and because you will have a little better understanding of what your mother went through all those years raising you, the two of you may grow closer as well during this time. In any case, it pays to be sensitive to the feelings of your mother, too.

Your Father

Your father is going through his own set of changes, which may be similar to what your mother is experiencing. Not every man or woman who becomes a parent is initially thrilled with the idea, And the same is true for grandparents. While they may love their grandchildren, some older people hate the idea of being called "Grandma" or "Grandpa" because it makes them feel ancient. For this reason and others, some grandparents never really develop much of a relationship with their grandkids.

On the other hand, your dad could be tickled pink about becoming a grandfather. In fact, he has been pestering you for years about having children and still wonders why it took you so long to get around to it. He can't wait to take the baby to the park and buy him a scooter when he's old enough and fly kites with him. But change diapers? Nah, that's your job, son.

FACT

Of those grandparents who do not live with their grandchildren, nearly half still see their grandchildren every week. Another one-third or so see or speak to their grandkids on a monthly basis. But 12 percent of all grandparents seldom have contact with their grandchildren, only talking on the phone or seeing them in person once every two or three months.

Accepting Help

Because having a baby represents such a huge transition in your life—not only for you and your partner, but your family and friends as well—you may feel a certain amount of stress. This stress need not be overwhelming. Your family and friends are actually a tremendous resource. Once you come to accept this (and it does take time), your relations with them may go more smoothly.

Your family and in-laws may be as loony as they come. They may be bossy and intrusive at times. They may be a royal pain in the you-know-what. But most assuredly they want to be useful and help you. Here are some jobs they can do:

- Go with your partner on a doctor's visit if you can't make it.
- Be on the lookout for good deals on baby gear and clothes.
- Help you paint the nursery or build the crib.
- Help you financially by hiring a once-a-month cleaning service or diaper service.
- Assist you with the birth (talk to your partner before you make this offer to anyone).
- Help you make phone calls to people after the baby is born.
- Cook meals ahead of time for you to stick in the freezer and eat after the baby comes.

Because they are eager to help, your family and friends will generally be happy and grateful to do the things you ask. As you will find as you get closer and closer to the due date, it is hard to sit around and wait. Having things to do will make the waiting easier for everyone.

Feelings of Isolation

It is possible, of course, that in the midst of all this family togetherness, with all these giddy feelings of expectation for the baby on the way, someone may feel left out. That someone may be you. You may feel like an outsider even in the middle of a joyous family celebration.

Things have changed in your life, and you're not entirely thrilled about it. You used to hang out with your buddies after work and that isn't happening so much anymore. And when the baby arrives, you get this uneasy feeling in the pit of your stomach that isn't going to happen ever again.

QUOTE

Dr. Edwin Hoffman-Smith, a father and family physician, has an interesting idea for helping men come to grips with their feelings during this life-shifting time: writing in a journal. "Being a father is a huge part of how men view themselves," he says. "Journaling can help fathers, especially new fathers, come to terms with how they feel about the changes their lives are undergoing."

Even as some of your friends are steadily receding from your social circle, your extended family—hers and yours—is coming forward to fill the gap. Frankly, you may not be too thrilled about that one, either. It seems like you've seen your mother-in-law and some of your partner's friends more in the past six months than you ever did before. And what do they all talk about? Baby, baby, baby.

Maybe you realize intellectually that you're not irrelevant—that your partner does, in fact, need you, and your baby, when he comes, will need you too. And you recognize that it is right and good that all these other people are excited about the baby. You're excited too—you really are—but still, there is no denying it: at times you feel isolated and alone, merely a spectator to this grand parade passing by.

Coping Strategies

There is a lot of stress that comes with being a pregnant father. You have a lot to think about, a lot to plan, and a lot of changes to absorb in what seems like an awfully short time. New demands are coming at you from your partner and family. Meanwhile, you may already be working harder to make more money for when the baby arrives.

Some of these pressures are real and need to be addressed, such as money, but some of the stresses you're feeling may be self-induced. Since you've never had a baby before, you don't know what to expect. This may make you put more pressure on yourself than you really need to.

Exercise Is the Way

Exercise is a proven method of controlling stress. The reason for this is simple—it works. You're going to feel better about yourself and your situation after you spend an hour in the gym, go for a jog, or take a ten-mile bike ride. Whatever you do to get your head on straight, do it. And keep doing it, as regularly as you can.

Pregnancy changes your world, but it is nothing like what will happen after the baby arrives. Once she arrives, you have very little time to do anything, including exercise. For now, you still have a great deal of freedom and free time, comparatively speaking, so take advantage of both while you can.

Go Out with the Guys

Okay, so maybe it's not exactly the way it used to be with you and your friends. But you're a guy and, as such you still have to blow off a little steam now and then. Even Mr. Dependability gets to take a night off, and there's no reason you shouldn't get to as well.

Go out and howl at the moon with your buddies, if you've got the itch to do that. See a movie your partner has no interest in. Watch a game from your favorite sports bar. Pick something that you haven't been able to do in a while and plan on an evening out. If your partner is very understanding, make plans to get away from everything. Take a day or two off from work and get the guys together for a long weekend in the mountains.

Your partner will understand. She may even encourage you to go. Just because she is tired and feels like staying home doesn't mean you always have to do the same.

ESSENTIAL

Be aware of the due date before you schedule your getaway. This is also true for travel at work. You need to stay close to the home front for at least one and perhaps two months before the baby is due. Neither you nor your partner will be comfortable with you out of town too near the time that the baby is due.

Keep Things Normal

Another way to manage stress is to take the opposite approach. Instead of going on a big getaway, keep things as normal as possible. Stick to your regular routine, as long as your routine works for you.

Although the regular workday routine can sometimes be a grind, it can also provide a great deal of comfort for the father-to-be. Driving to work, putting in your eight hours, doing your job, seeing the people you see there, and driving back home at the end of the day can provide parents-to-be a solid foundation in a world that feels like it is constantly shifting.

Think Positive

Your family, which once consisted almost exclusively of you and your partner, is now a much more crowded place. Like it or not, so many more people are part of it, and that includes this kid you've never met and who's still being formed, but who is already causing extreme amounts of mischief. There is nothing you can do about this, really.

What you can do, amid the hubbub, is keep a positive attitude. These changes, you will find, are not so bad after all. Everything is going to be just fine. This is your world, and welcome to it.

Part of what it means to be a father is learning how to adjust to this new, suddenly expanding world—a world that includes your family and friends and your partner's family and friends. While some people are stepping back, others are coming forward in your life. Some changes have already occurred, with plenty more to come. And all of this is occurring because of a tiny little being you haven't even met yet.

CHAPTER 6

Common Fears

Pregnancy is a physical and emotional experience for women. But for men, after they help create the baby, there is no physical side. The growth they experience is internal. This chapter discusses some of the emotional and mental hurdles that men must deal with on the road to fatherhood.

Your Feelings Are Normal

The variety of emotions that most fathers-to-be experience are normal and natural. Every man feels a variety of emotions during pregnancy, and there is nothing wrong with this. It is just part of being human.

Still, many fathers-to-be do not like to admit that they feel doubt or worry or fear about what lies ahead. There are good reasons for this reluctance. Men intuitively understand that their job during pregnancy is different from their partner's and know that a lot of unnecessary emotion on their part is not going to help them do that job.

Men need to be steady and solid and reliable during this time of change. The father-to-be wants to deliver in the clutch and be the cool man in a crisis. He needs to be there for his partner and come through for her. He intuitively knows that what he *feels* at this time is not nearly as important as what he *does*.

QUOTE

"Don't neglect your fears; listen to them and work through them," advises Jerrold Lee Shapiro, a psychologist and father of two. "One of the best fear breakers is to talk to other guys you know, especially new fathers who've been through it. 'If Chuck can get through it, I can get through it.' That sort of idea." And, says Shapiro, talking about these things will help ease your worries.

Another reason a man may shy away from expressing or even admitting these feelings is that he know his needs are secondary to his partner's and the baby's. For many men, having any doubts or worries at all seems like a kind of betrayal. It feels like an admission of weakness or a sign that he may not be up to the job he is supposed to and sincerely wants to do. Some men are embarrassed to have these feelings and do not like talking about them.

One could argue, though, that feelings like doubt, worry, and even fear are a sign that you are preparing yourself emotionally to do the job at hand. Accepting and understanding your feelings may help you do a better job as a father, not a worse one. It may also help to know that virtually every father before you has experienced feelings similar to yours. But they made it through, and so can you.

Passing Out in the Delivery Room

One of the most popular television shows of all time was *The Cosby Show*, which was the top-rated program for many years and can still be seen in reruns. Starring Bill Cosby as an obstetrician, the show often featured scenes that took place in a hospital delivery room, with women in labor and babies being born.

Almost invariably, the fathers-to-be on *The Cosby Show* were shown as bumbling fools who fainted during childbirth. Another running joke was the father-to-be forgetting what he needed to do when his partner went into labor. They'd run around like idiots before jumping in the car and screeching off to the hospital. When they arrived, someone would point out that they'd forgotten to bring the person who was actually having the baby, and they'd sheepishly climb back in the car to go get their wives.

The Cosby Show, as retro as it is, resembles many television shows and movies today in the way it depicts fathers-to-be. The man-who-faints-during-childbirth bit is still a popular comedy staple. Despite its popularity in comedy, this almost never happens in real life.

Not Being Able to Provide

There is a sound and sensible reason for fathers-to-be to worry during pregnancy: there are things to worry about. With the possible exception of passing out in the delivery room, these worries are not just in your head or media disseminated fictions; they are grounded in objective reality. With a baby on the way, certain things need to be done, and one of the chief worries for both expectant fathers and mothers is, plain and simple, money.

Doing the Financial Math

You don't have to be a genius to figure it out; you just have to do the math. When it was just you and your partner, you had two incomes supporting two people. When a baby enters the picture, you will have two incomes supporting three people.

But wait a second—somebody is going to have to take care of that baby. Either you will have to pay for child care, which is certainly not cheap, or one of you will have to stay home. That somebody, almost always, is Mom.

How long she stays off work is a thorny question, and the answer varies from family to family, but she will likely be off work for a period of time. This may reduce her income, changing the financial math once more.

FACT

Expectant parents worry about money because it directly affects how much time they will be able to spend with their child. This holds true for both women and men. A national survey found that 65 percent of all fathers said they would spend more time with their children if they could afford to do it.

Instead of having two incomes supporting two people, you have one income—probably yours—supporting three people. No wonder you're worried. It is the most reasonable thing in the world for a man to have concerns during this time about supporting his family.

The Emotional Nature of Money

Worry is beneficial to some degree since it may be an indication that you need to take action in a given area. On the other hand, too much worry may hurt you and perhaps even prevent you from acting. All this is complicated—made more worrisome, if you will—by the emotional nature of money.

Some people will say money is merely a matter of dollars and cents, strictly a bottom-line issue. While this may be true when you are running a business, it is seldom the case with a family. This is particularly true when you have a baby because how you feel about money is so often connected to your own (and your partner's) childhood and upbringing. For instance, if you didn't have much material comfort when you were growing up, you may be determined to give your child what you never had, even if you can't always afford to.

There are practical steps you can take to ease your worries over money. They require some advance planning, perhaps some hard thinking which may force some hard choices, and a sit-down or two with your partner to talk it all over. These steps will all be discussed in greater detail in Chapters 7, 8, and 9.

Is It Really My Child?

One of the things that some men think about is whether or not the child is actually theirs. Although these men wonder if they are the child's real father, few talk about their worry openly. It's just something that gnaws at the pit of their stomach.

In most cases, this is a baseless worry. Intellectually, you know that you are, of course, the father. This is, once more, a reminder of how different it is to be a father than a mother. There can be no doubt who the mother is; the baby is growing inside her. But dear old Dad? Sometimes even after the baby is born and the man can see his physical characteristics reflected in the child, he may still continue to have doubts.

While a father-to-be might have these worries, he is probably also insulted by the very idea that his partner had an affair. He does not believe the woman carrying his child has been cheating, and he is hurt by this insinuation. It's more likely that his worry stems from the fact that many men are simply overwhelmed by the idea that they helped create a baby, that they participated in something so monumental as to cause another human being to be born. This causes them to doubt themselves and their own child's paternity.

Aging and Mortality

Having a baby can bring out issues in your life that maybe you were ignoring or in denial about. One of those issues is your age. Suddenly, you feel a lot older than you did only months ago thanks to the baby on his way. Why is that? Part of it has to do with the fact that your role in life is changing radically, and with this change you are being forced to look at yourself in a new way.

From Son to Father

All your life you have been somebody's son. Being a son implies youth, starting out on life's journey, and, to a certain degree, being protected by your parents. While you are still a son to your parents, the coming arrival of your own child has you taking on a new role—that of father. Being a father has different associations, and it comes with different responsibilities.

The man who has become a father, without doubt, has greater duties than the man who is a son. The father must provide for his family. He must sacrifice his own desires to their desires and needs. He is a teacher, a disciplinarian, and a role model.

One of the most obvious differences between a father and a son is age. When you are a son, you hardly think about time because you feel you have so much of it, so much that you can waste it. The father has a different view. He has lived in the world a little bit and absorbed its hard knocks. For him, time is in short supply. It is too precious to waste.

A Sense of Mortality

These thoughts and feelings about age and growing older occur naturally to every man when he is about to become a father. After the baby comes, these feelings only intensify, in part because they reflect reality. Each birthday the baby celebrates means that not only is he another year older, but you are too. Time speeds up when you become a parent.

Your child now occupies your former position—the young, protected one who is just beginning life's journey. Your role has switched to that of provider, protector, teacher, and role model. If somebody has to make a sacrifice for the betterment of the family, it is going to be you (or your partner) who has to bite the bullet and do it.

QUESTION

Is something wrong with me if I don't have these feelings?
Not at all. Some men feel these issues strongly, while others hardly ever think about them and then only in passing. Each man's experience of fatherhood is unique to him, even though many of these experiences and feelings are universal.

Your own parents may or may not be living. Whatever the case, in becoming a father you have a changed view of your own mortality. Before, as a son, your own father or parents stood between you and the ultimate mystery. In the natural order of things—although things, of course, do not always follow this order—they would die before you. This was only one of the ways in which you felt protected by them.

But with a child on the way, the old order is being rearranged. It's like the children's game of musical chairs: your baby has taken your former chair and you have moved into a chair that signifies being one step closer to done with the game. It's a sobering realization.

Becoming Like Dad

When you become a parent (or a parent-to-be), you will receive a ton of advice from many well-meaning people—friends, family, and sometimes even complete strangers. You will listen to the doctors and medical specialists. You will read books and attend childbirth preparation classes. But the biggest influence on how you will raise your children is already part of your psyche.

How were you raised as a child? What was it like when you were growing up? How did your parents handle things? All of your childhood issues, whatever they are, will resurface when you become a parent. This will also hold true for your partner, who will be grappling with similar issues relating to her own childhood and parents.

Your chief role model for being a father was your own father. You learned lessons from him on how to be a man and a father, whether you are conscious of these lessons or not. You must now deal with these lessons, no matter how good or bad they were, when you yourself become a father.

The Bad Father

Let's face it. Not all dads are good guys. NFL coach and former Chicago Bears middle linebacker Mike Singletary is an active Christian who promotes responsibility among men. One day he went to a women's prison to speak. The warden warned him to expect an unfriendly reception from the female inmates. "Why is that?" Singletary asked. "Because you're a man and a father," said the warden, "and in almost every case, the one person who has caused the most pain in all of these inmates' lives is their father."

Some fathers do bad things to their children and their partners. Some desert their families. Some cause so much trouble and misery that it is better for everyone involved if they simply leave the house and never come back.

Your father may have done rotten things to you. In the back of your mind you may be thinking, "Does that mean I'm going to do rotten things too? Is that what it means to be a father—to never be around, and then on those few times when you're around, to scold your children constantly and cause misery? Am I going to be like him?"

The Good Father

The opposite role model is the good father. This is the man who could do no wrong, who always acted for the good of his family. The good father is strong but caring, a thoughtful, patient person who dispenses nuggets of wisdom to his children that they carry with them all their lives. Think of some of the old-time television sitcom dads whose shows still air on cable: Andy Griffith, Dick Van Dyke, and of course Ward Cleaver of *Leave It to Beaver*. (Of course, Homer Simpson might not fit into this category.)

You may have a dad somewhat like this—a guy you looked up to, perhaps even idolized. Because he was such a great role model, you may think to yourself, "How can I ever be as good a father? How can I ever live up to the standards he set?" And these sorts of thoughts may make you uneasy.

Becoming Your Own Man

Like the bad father, the good father may only exist in your memory or perception. The reality may be that your father had both good and bad points. He was a flawed man, perhaps, who made mistakes but did the best he could given his circumstances and the times in which he lived. Remember that your own dad, for all his faults, was once a guy who, like yourself, had to make the transition into fatherhood. His own father (and mother) may not have been the greatest role models in the world, either.

When you become a parent, you become more sympathetic and understanding of your own parents. You realize what a hard job they had. It's impossible to do or say the right thing at every given moment with your children. Nevertheless, it is important to recognize that when you become a father, you *can* follow your own path and make your own choices.

Be aware. Make conscious choices. Check your motives to make sure you are acting because you truly think what you are doing is the right thing. Some parents-to-be think things should be done a certain way simply because that is how it was done when they were children.

Will My Relationship Be Hurt?

Both men and women worry about how a baby will affect their relationship. For this reason, many couples put off getting pregnant for many years. They do not want a child to affect what they have together as a couple or all the things they want to do.

As the divorce rates show, these worries are anything but groundless. A child puts stress on a relationship. Here are only a few of the stresses that come with having a child:

- Less free time
- Less time for anything but the baby
- Less romantic time
- More money worries
- More exhaustion
- More in-law involvement
- More demands on you
- More potential sources of disagreement

It is possible that just your partner's becoming pregnant has added new friction points in your relationship that were not there before. You may have already noticed that you have less free time because you feel the need to get home to tend to your partner's needs. Your in-laws may be calling and coming over more. Other stresses may be popping up. What you are feeling will only increase once the baby arrives.

Concerns about Your Partner

Labor and delivery are not without risk, and this is why most couples choose to give birth in a hospital. If something unexpected happens to either mother or child, they are surrounded by medical professionals who can give them immediate attention. Lives may truly hang in the balance.

For men, another aspect of the process is watching their partner endure so much pain, for so long. It is difficult to see the woman you love go through such great hardship, and there is little you can do about it except encourage her verbally and moisten her forehead with a wet washcloth. Women giving birth have also been known to single out the person who got them into this position—uh, that's you—and subject him to a terrible tongue-lashing, screaming and cursing at him in language that would embarrass a longshoreman. While this doesn't happen often, it has certainly been known to occur.

This is hard to take—seeing your partner in so much pain and hearing her swear at you. Even so, men should realize that their burden is far, far, far lighter than the one being carried by the woman. If it were somehow magically possible for fathers to trade places with mothers, letting them carry a baby to term and then give birth, most men would politely but respectfully decline the offer.

Concerns about Baby

Again, as with so many of the other worries and fears discussed in this chapter, there is a reason to be concerned about your baby. It's possible that something could go wrong. That is why you and your partner are learning everything you can about this event, and why so many trained people—doctors, nurses, nurse-midwives, specialists, professional labor assistants—are going to be involved in helping it come off safely.

FACT

By about the third month, the fetus has fingers and toes with soft nails. By the next month, she has fingerprints and toe prints. By the sixth month her movements have become strong and coordinated, and her hands sometimes grip the umbilical cord. The sixth month is also about the time when a baby can survive outside her mother's body in intensive care.

You can also feel reassured by the many medical tests and screens that your partner is undergoing. Still, even with all these procedures (which are not foolproof), you may worry that your child will not turn out "normal" in some way. When no one is looking, many new fathers count their child's toes and fingers once she's born to make sure she has them all.

Adoption Concerns

Men and women who adopt children also encounter lots of stresses before that moment when their new child comes home and becomes part of their family. Sometimes they already have biological children, and so there are natural worries about how this new child will relate to others in the family, and vice versa. The adopted child does not physically resemble his parents or siblings. Will other people notice the difference, gossip about it, ask questions?

Sometimes your parents or grandparents may disapprove of adopting a child from another country or a different heritage. There may be racial or cultural issues involved.

All of this may make you and your partner feel awful, or even inferior somehow. Because of some trick of biology or genetics, you cannot have a baby together. Meanwhile your brother and his wife have four children. Why him but not you?

Adopting a child (like trying to conceive one through artificial insemination) can be a struggle at times. You can get your hopes up and then have your heart broken in the most sudden way. All the while you may be wondering to yourself: will I bond with this child who is not of my own flesh and blood?

Take heart, Dad. Almost certainly, you will. Almost certainly, you will fall in love with your child as surely as other parents fall in love with their children. But it is all right to ask such questions, and have such concerns.

Getting Support

Your concerns are not just in your head and you need not feel ashamed of them. They are not a sign of weakness. Every father-to-be feels these things. Likewise, the doubts you may have about yourself are similar to what other fathers-to-be are feeling and what other fathers before you have felt when they went through this process.

Even if they're chewing their fingernails off with worry, many men do not want to admit that they are experiencing doubts or worries about the pregnancy. Even if they will cop to a niggling doubt or two, they figure they can handle it on their own without asking for help. This may be true; you may not need a shoulder to lean on. If you do, though, there are places where you can find support that will apply to all types of new fathers and fathers-to-be.

Finding a Sympathetic Ear

One good place to start is with somebody who has been through it before—your brother, perhaps, or a close friend. He may make a joke at the start because revealing his feelings puts him in a vulnerable position too, but once he sees that you're serious and willing to open up to him, he will almost certainly let down his guard as well.

It may not be necessary for this person to be a father or, for that matter, another man. You may have a close woman friend and feel more comfortable talking to her. Many men find it easier to talk to women because they tend to listen better and do not feel the need to tell you what to do or immediately offer solutions.

You may be more comfortable talking to people you don't know as well, such as the men's support group that meets at your church or local community center. These men have probably gone through what you're going through, and they will be sympathetic to what you are experiencing.

Another obvious outlet is the Internet. You can sometimes have pretty candid e-mail discussions with friends and family and never set eyes on them or talk to them. Social networking sites such as Facebook and Twitter offer more possibilities. You can find numerous chat rooms for fathers on websites devoted to parenting. If you wish, you can get involved in discussions with other fathers and get things off your chest without anyone knowing who you are.

Professional Help

If you feel overwhelmed or troubled by your impending fatherhood, why not talk to a professional about it? There is no harm in seeking advice, and it may do a world of good. You can talk to a professional therapist or your priest or minister. Your talk will be kept private, and you will receive the sympathetic ear you need.

The great thing about talking about these concerns is that the talk alone may prove therapeutic. You are dealing with emotions, and because of this there may be no specific solution to your given concern. Luckily, you will often feel better simply because you got to talk about it.

Talking to Your Partner

Surely the best person to confide in is your partner, the mother of your child. But she may be so wrapped up with the child inside her that she hasn't really thought about you. She may be surprised that you have such feelings. At first she may even be dismissive of your concerns and feel that you are being selfish and thinking only of yourself.

If this occurs, ask for a time when you can both talk. Let her talk fully, and when she is done, take your turn. She may be more willing to listen to you once she feels her concerns have been heard.

Of course, it is highly possible that your partner is genuinely interested in your interior life. She may be secretly concerned about you. She may feel you drifting away from her emotionally and wonder if you are having second thoughts about the whole situation. The chance to talk may relieve her greatly and give peace of mind to you both.

CHAPTER 7

The Economics of Having a Baby

Money is a prime concern for couples expecting a baby thanks to all the arguments and stress it can cause. This chapter will cover the basics of money management and includes topics like why it is important to set family priorities, the credit traps you need to avoid, and strategies you can use to reduce your worries and increase your sense of security.

Money Worries

It has been said that the arguments between couples tend to focus on two main areas: sex and money. Sex will be discussed in Chapter 11. As for money, it is certainly understandable that cash would be something both men and women would worry and occasionally fight about during this sensitive time. The economics of having a baby can seem awfully scary; indeed, that is why many couples put off becoming parents in the first place. They feel they cannot afford it.

You and your partner have probably been paying the bills on two incomes, yours and hers. With a baby on the way, you are looking ahead to the time when your partner will stop working for an undetermined period both before and after the birth. That means that the three of you will likely be living on your income alone, at least for a while.

Mom's Point of View

In Chapter 9, you will learn ways that you and your partner can soften the financial blow during this time. As soon as you learn she is pregnant, you need to check in on how much paid vacation leave you've accrued at work. Although you probably did pay attention to how much paid leave you have, you need to really focus on this amount now because you will need this time when the baby comes and possibly before. Your partner will need to research her company or organization's paid time off and medical leave policies to see which fits best for your family. You may also be able to draw from your personal savings.

All of this will help, but it may not entirely ease her mind. She may have worked and collected a paycheck every week of her adult life since leaving school, but now that she's pregnant, she's in a more vulnerable spot than she's been in for a long time. She knows she will not be on the job for a while, and that during this period she will be caring for the baby. To some degree, depending on how you two have worked things out, she may be dependent on you financially.

Your Point of View

As much as you'd like to reassure her on this score, you have worries of your own. In fact, you may even have lost sleep over it. You've done the math over and over in your head, and you've come to the conclusion that you just can't do it. There is simply no way that you can afford to have a baby at this time.

Unfortunately, it's too late; the baby's on the way and there's no turning back. You think about ways that you can make more money. Can you ask for a raise? No way, you're not up for a salary review until next year and business isn't the greatest right now, anyhow.

What about looking for a better job? That's a possibility, but it takes time. Get a second job? That's another option, one many fathers and fathers-to-be decide is right for them.

Losing Your Job

Now, that's a fine kettle of fish, isn't it? You find out you're going to be a father, you've got things all lined up the way you want—and then suddenly you get laid off or lose your job for some reason.

Obviously, the first thing is to get down to the unemployment office if you qualify, do the paperwork, and get those checks coming in. The second thing is to try and relax. There are other jobs out there for you, even if they may not be exactly what you want at this time. Update the resume, start making phone calls, get your name and face out there, and stay positive.

QUOTE

"My advice for any dad who is an unemployed father and husband is to just have faith and keep calm through the storm," says Travis Roste, father of two who once lost his job as a shipping clerk. "When I doubt myself the most, I just take a minute to imagine the future a year or two from now. I always know without a doubt that I will be employed somewhere, earning a paycheck, coming home to my incredible family."

That is the main thing is to keep your attitude strong. Don't freak out because there's a baby on the way. In fact, let the baby serve as an inspiration for you. You are not going to let her down. You and your partner will find a way to make it, no matter what, and everything will be fine.

The Way It Goes

It may be reassuring to know that practically every other father and father-to-be in the world worries about money. Unless you've got a million bucks in the bank, it is reasonable to have such concerns. You worry about your job and your financial stability just as you worry about the health of your child and partner during childbirth.

Keep in mind that nobody has a handle on these issues right away and that they take time to figure out. You may not have every detail completely planned before the baby arrives. New issues will pop up that you hadn't planned on when the munchkin finally appears, so expect to feel financial pressures and worries for as long as you raise children.

Money: It's a Family Affair

One thing to realize is that the money burden is not all on your shoulders. Even if you make more money than she does, are the chief provider, and feel strongly in your heart that this is your most important role and the way that you can best contribute to your family's well-being, this is not your problem alone. Finances are a shared responsibility, and you and your partner need to face these issues together.

FACT

Each year for the past two decades, a national polling firm has conducted surveys about how men view themselves and their role in the family. Fathers have consistently said that "being a good provider" is their top job—ahead of being a leader, decision-maker, or anything else.

Look at this way. You're sharing more of the household chores, right? You're cooking more and doing some of the food shopping. You're going with your partner to her obstetrician appointments and planning to be the birth coach. When the baby comes home, you're going to be elbow to elbow with your partner, changing diapers, fixing bottles, and doing whatever needs to be done. Your partner can share some of the financial responsibilities in the same way you're helping out in these areas.

She is thinking a lot about money issues too and has her own set of worries. Because of this, she may be willing to sit down with you at the kitchen table and talk.

The Emotions of Money

It is customary for financial experts to talk about money as if it is merely a matter of dollars and cents. While this may be true when you are preparing a profit and loss statement for a business, it is definitely not the case when you are dealing with families, especially families with a baby on the way. Emotions come into play. This is why figuring out household finances can sometimes be such a knotty affair; there are so many more issues to deal with than just money alone.

How You Were Raised

When you have a baby, your own childhood and the way you were raised will greatly influence how you act as a parent. Did you grow up with plenty, or was there a feeling that there was never enough? Were your parents fair? Did they play favorites with you or any of your brothers and sisters?

Perhaps you were an only child. Because of this, you may want to have only one child yourself. Of course, the reverse may also be true and you may want to have a big family so your children will have siblings you never had.

If you did not have something as a child, you may feel strongly that you must give this thing you lacked to your child. This could be virtually anything: money, toys, a big house, a college education, or love. By the same token, if you had a rich abundance as a child, you may be determined to provide the same bounty to your offspring.

ALERT

Your partner may be focused inwardly on the baby and not thinking about money as much as you are. Talking about it may initially scare or intimidate her. She may feel defensive. Reassure her by explaining that you simply feel the need to check in with her and stay in sync on this important subject that concerns you both.

How Your Partner Was Raised

You bring a certain amount of emotional baggage into parenthood. This holds true for your partner as well, and her baggage isn't the same as yours. Always keep this in mind when you talk with her about money. You both may work up a great deal of emotional heat on topics that, from a strictly financial point of view, are relatively unimportant, but these issues lie at the core of how you see yourself as a parent and your expectations for your child.

Your partner had her own unique childhood experiences. These experiences, whether positive or negative, will help shape her view about how money should be spent, just as your childhood informs your view. Here are some other non-dollars-and-cents issues that may arise in your discussions:

- Your values—what you believe is right for your child
- Your expectations—what you expect to occur
- Your image of parenthood—what it is supposed to be like
- Your expectations of your partner—your partner's view of your role as father and your view of her as mother
- Peer pressure—what other parents do with their children
- Family pressure—what your parents or other family members think should occur

Some of the expectations you have about raising children are formed out of your own experience. Other people's experiences and what they have told you will also play a role. Television programs and the media may have led you to create some unrealistic expectations of what family life is like. All of this will emerge when you talk about the often emotionally volatile subject of money.

FACT

One recent behavioral study showed that men in all cultures listed "beauty" as the chief reason they are attracted to a partner. For women, however, a man's top attraction is his ability to be a provider. Consequently, even if women contribute substantially to household income, working mothers nearly always expect fathers to earn money too.

Setting Your Priorities

There are no easy answers to all of these money questions, and every family works out financial issues in their own way. What works for one family may not work for another, but every family needs to establish priorities to determine how they spend their money.

You may not have ever talked to your partner about your financial priorities. Nevertheless, both of you demonstrate your priorities every day without saying a word to each other or anyone else. At the end of each month, take a look at how you spent your money. That will tell you all about what your priorities are.

What can be upsetting about learning that you are about to become a father is the discovery that you may have to change your spending priorities. In some cases, a minor tuneup may not be enough; your habits may need a complete overhaul. Your partner may feel the same way. Something has got to change—or else.

Strategies for Getting Money

Stripped of their emotions (which is, admittedly, hard to do), the economics of pregnancy are like the economics of everyday life. Quite simply, you need to make more money than you spend. If you are not able to do this—and many new parents are not—you need to find ways to cover the shortfall. There are a variety of methods you can use to help.

Use the Resources You Have

As mentioned earlier, many fathers-to-be and fathers take second jobs to build their savings or pay off bills. You may have paid vacation leave from your job that represents a sort of time savings bank that you can dip into as the need arises.

Do you own your home? You may be able to take out a second mortgage or a home equity line of credit that will supply you with cash. This cash can buy you or your wife time with baby. Be careful, though—your home is your greatest financial asset, now and in the future. When you establish a line of credit or a second mortgage you are, in effect, selling a long-term asset for short-term reasons. You may decide that the trade-off is worth it if your partner has her heart set on staying at home with the baby for an extended amount of time.

ALERT

Be "risk averse" during the pregnancy. Do not make any big spending or investment decisions. You have enough things on your mind as it is. After the baby comes and you get settled into this new life, then you can review your overall financial picture and see what needs to be done to improve it.

Another possibility is to sell something of value, such as one of your classic cars gathering dust in the garage or your baseball card collection languishing in a shoebox. A resource like this, if you are willing to part with it, is another way to produce extra cash until your partner goes back to work and finances are on a more even keel.

Borrowing or Receiving Money as a Gift

Your parents or your wife's parents may be able to help you financially and may even offer to help without you asking. They know the financial pressures you're under because they themselves faced similar pressures when they were new parents. They've come to a point in their lives where they are better able to help their children and grandchildren, and will probably be happy to do so.

If they cannot afford to give you money, they may be willing to front you a short-term loan. This is better than borrowing money from a bank, getting a cash advance on your credit card, or taking out a home equity line of credit, all loans you must pay back with interest. Even if your parents charge you interest, it will be nothing like the terms a bank will demand. Also, your family is not going to take your house away or put a lien on your paycheck if you have trouble paying the money back on time.

Pride may stop you from asking for or accepting money from your parents or relatives. You also may not want them to get tangled up in your financial affairs, and they may put strings on their gift or loan. As always, you will need to weigh the cost of receiving this money against the advantages that come from taking it.

Credit Card Debt

It is going to be difficult to get ahead financially if you carry exorbitant credit card debt. The more debt you incur, the bigger the hole you are digging for yourself. Paying that interest fee to the bank every month to service that debt is like throwing money away or adding more dirt in the hole that you must ultimately dig out.

FACT

If you owe $8,000 on a credit card that charges 18 percent interest, and you pay the minimum payment due of $160 each month, you will be free of this debt in ninety-four months—nearly eight years. The total interest charges you pay will be close to $6,900. Raising your monthly payment to $250, however, will erase the debt in forty-four months and cost you about $3,000 in interest.

New parents generally understand this, but again, the emotions come into play. Your partner's dream may be to have the perfect little nursery. In her mind, this requires a total makeover of the baby's room: new crib, new furniture, new paint job, new everything. You don't have the money to pay for it, so you pull out the plastic.

One thing you can do, if you have to go this route, is shop around among the credit card companies for one with lower interest rates than what you pay now. Some cards offer better deals than others, and the difference can save you money. As always, you need to be careful. If the economy is going through a rough patch and your job status is shaky (or you're unemployed), don't put yourself out on a limb by taking on too much debt.

Baby Expenses

The largest expenses that come with having a baby are the medical and hospital costs. If these are being paid for by your (or your partner's) health coverage from work, congratulations. You have saved yourself a ton of money. Nowadays, though, more and more medical providers are asking for a co-payment from couples—$500 or more—for the costs incurred at the hospital for labor and delivery services.

Additionally, you might decide to hire a professional labor assistant, or "doula." This is a nonmedical person whose job is to support you and your partner at the time of birth. A doula's fee, which comes out of your pocket, can range from $300 to $1500, with most doulas charging roughly in the middle of those two figures. For a home birth, you will likely need to hire a licensed midwife. Aside from the birth itself, you have other expenses to plan for, including:

- Car seat
- Baby clothes
- Stroller
- Baby sling or carrier
- Bassinet and crib
- Clothes dresser
- Nursery preparations and decorating
- Changing table
- Bouncy seat and other baby accessories
- Disposable diapers or diaper service

Note that several of these items are optional and you certainly do not need to buy everything new. You can save money by picking up second-hand items at garage sales and baby consignment shops, as well as by borrowing things. You may know plenty of other parents who don't need their stroller or baby backpack any longer. If you are using family heirlooms or hand-me-downs, make sure that they conform to current safety standards. Cribs and car seats, in particular, need to be carefully checked.

Getting Help

Having a baby does not need to bankrupt you. Think twice before going into debt to buy a bunch of new stuff. If you do, you are doing a disservice both to your child and yourself. You are going to have to pay for those things at some point. This will force you to spend more time on the job, meaning you will have less time with your family as a result.

Having a child brings up lots of emotions. If you and your partner can discuss and deal with some of these emotional issues, you may not need to run up your credit card bills. Remember, you're spending this money on a little person you've never met, who, frankly, does not care if she gets changed on a brand-new deluxe changing table or a rubber pad on top of a dresser.

Financial Advice

It may make sense for you to see a financial advisor or brokerage representative. Set a meeting time that is convenient for both you and your partner.

A financial advisor can review your situation and provide counsel on both your immediate present as well as the future. He may look critically at how you spend your money. He may give you advice as simple as shifting your funds from a bank checking account to a money market account that pays slightly higher interest. He will almost certainly talk to you about investing for your and your child's future. For more on investing strategies, see Chapter 8.

ALERT

Professional financial advisors work on a fee-for-service basis or by commission based on the investments they sell. You do not need to invest in anything at this moment. Even if you pay an up-front fee for an advisor's services, the best thing you can get from one right now may simply be information.

Credit Counseling

It is as hard to change long-time spending habits as it is to stop smoking or drinking. And with both you and your partner earning good salaries, there may have been no reason to change. Everything may have been going fine until she got pregnant and you both had to take a hard look at how you were going to swing this whole deal, money-wise. You may have come to the realization that you are digging a hole for yourself and the hole is only getting deeper.

You may have lost your job and be forced to pay medical expenses out of pocket. You may have forgotten to plan for your partner's loss of income during pregnancy. You may have underestimated the costs involved in having a baby. Any or all of these things could have happened, causing you to go thousands of dollars in debt.

Don't beat yourself up about it; these things happen. Nonprofit consumer credit agencies around the country can provide counseling and help you develop a plan to reduce your debt and spending. Check the phone book or conduct an Internet search for a list of offices in your area.

Every couple worries about money when they are about to have a baby. These worries can trigger intense emotions, emotions that touch on your image of yourself as a parent and your expectations for you and your child. Realizing this, you and your partner need to talk about your priorities and values. Once you are clear about what comes first, the question of what you need to do with your money—whether to spend less, pay down debt, or save more—will become much clearer, too.

CHAPTER 8

Long-Term Financial Issues

When you become a father, you need to think both short- and long-term. You need adequate income for the immediate present, but you cannot completely ignore the future—yours or your family's. Here are some financial planning issues to think about for the months ahead.

Why Your Perspective Is Valuable

Sometimes men feel left out of their partner's pregnancy. All the focus is on her and the baby, so they're not sure how they fit in or how they can be useful. One of the ways you can be useful is to do some thinking and planning about money.

Your partner may be a planner at heart, and the two of you may have already sat down at the kitchen table, calculator in hand. Maybe you've already printed out your spending and income statements for the year. Your pencils may be worn to the nub from plotting out your financial situation for the next year. Chances are, though, she is a little distracted with this baby growing bigger and bigger inside her, and she has a whole bunch of things on her mind besides money.

ALERT

Always keep talking with your partner—about money and everything else. This is the wrong time to make any big decisions on spending or changing jobs without first consulting her. Just as you want to stay in tune with her pregnancy, keep her involved in your thinking and decision-making.

This is where you may be able to take the wheel and let her relax for a while. Your perspective on spending and finances is valuable. She will almost certainly welcome your ability to take the lead on these issues because it will mean one less thing she has to think about.

Buying a Bigger Vehicle: Pros and Cons

One of the things that happens when you learn you are going to be a father is that you look around at all the things in your life and realize how inadequate they are. What worked for two people is clearly not going to make it for three, especially when that third person is a baby. Baby changes everything, or so you think.

Your vehicles may become a sudden source of consternation. You just love that sporty little convertible two-seater of yours, but where are you going to put the baby? And your partner's old, broken-down sedan is ready to be put out to pasture. Does becoming a father mean you have to buy a larger vehicle?

The Family Monster-Mobile

If you have ever ventured into the parking lot of a preschool or grade school when all the moms are arriving to pick up their children, you might naturally think that in order to have a family these days, it is required that you own an SUV. It can be comical to watch tiny three- and four-year-olds who can't tie their shoelaces get strapped into the car seat of some giant house on wheels when you know it is only Mom and child roaring down the road to ballet or soccer practice.

Sport utility vehicles are popular with families because of their roominess, their carrying capacity, and the feeling of safety and security they provide. Another aspect of their appeal is their image as a rugged, outdoorsy, off-road vehicle. Men in particular seem to like this, although only a small percentage of SUV owners ever travel on anything but paved streets. Men also like being able to sit up high in a SUV because it allows them to see the road better and promotes safety.

Of course, SUVs do tend to consume copious amounts of gasoline, which is a problem not only for the environment but for the wallet as well. Hybrid vehicles that combine gasoline and electric technology are available for SUVs, crossovers, and a growing array of other models. When it comes time to buy a new car, hybrids are surely worth considering even though they are more expensive than standard gasoline models.

What Soccer Moms Drive

Another popular family mobile is the minivan, which is also a common sight wherever parents and children congregate. It was all the rage some years ago, but then it developed image problems. The minivan became what "soccer moms" drove, and as a result many men did not want to be seen behind the wheel of one. They preferred the more powerful, truck-like SUVs.

As a response to their dowdy image, minivans have become sleeker and more stylish in the hopes that they will appeal to men as well as women. For reasons of style and fuel economy, crossovers are becoming a popular choice. They are sort of "mini-SUVs" with the feel and handling more of a car than a truck and without the gas-guzzling stigma associated with the biggest SUVs. What attracts families to crossovers, minivans and SUVs is the same: lots of room inside to carry children.

Your Parents' Family Mobile

One more option to consider in terms of a family vehicle is the wagon or "combi-wagon" as they're sometimes called. Today's wagons are an update of the old-fashioned station wagon. Many baby boomers had parents who drove a wood-paneled Country Squire station wagon or something similar. When the baby boomers grew up and became parents themselves, they did not want to drive what their mother and father did. Out went the station wagon, and in came the minivan, SUV, crossover, and now, the station-less wagon.

Wagons have a smaller, sportier profile than an SUV and yet can offer considerable seating and hauling space. Today's sedans are also worth checking out since they can store lots of stuff in the trunk, fit a baby in the back seat, run economically, and get pretty good gas mileage. Of course, a sedan is not exactly a Vette, is it? Oh well, you'll adjust.

No Need to Buy Anything Now

Now that you are about to become a family man, one of these large vehicles may be in your future. Luckily, that doesn't mean you have to get rid of that zippy little convertible out front just yet.

ESSENTIAL

Before buying a car, think about your priorities. Do you want to add monthly car payments to your bills on top of everything else? If you've got the dough to swing it financially, more power to you. Given all the uncertainties that come with pregnancy and children, though, it is wiser to wait.

However you work it out, one thing is sure: you do not need to buy a new family vehicle at this time. Babies are small, and yours will almost certainly fit just fine into a car seat in the back seat of your current car. As time passes and you get a better sense of what you need and can afford, then you can think about perhaps getting a more family-friendly set of wheels.

Owning a Home

For most men and women, buying a house is the biggest financial investment they will ever make. They will likely take on large amounts of debt and pay a sizable monthly mortgage along with property taxes. Of course, unlike paying rent to a landlord, the house you buy may increase in value over the long-term, making your investment a sound one. (Although nothing is certain, as the sub-prime mortgage fiasco has showed. Housing prices can go down just as surely as they can go up.)

But a house is more than just a financial asset or an investment; it is where you live and where you are going to raise your kids. Buying a home means that you are putting down roots in a community, and this has psychological and spiritual significance. You are planting a flag, claiming this place as your own.

Home as Nest

The pressure to buy a house sometimes starts with pregnancy. You and your partner may be content living in an apartment, but with a baby on the way the apartment style of living no longer seems adequate. You feel the need to get more space, perhaps to have a lawn or a backyard. You may wish to get a jump on things and try to get into a better school district for your child when the time comes.

Many couples put off having a child until they can get into a house of their own. The reason for this often has to do with people's memories of childhood—how they were raised. They grew up in a house, not an apartment, and they want the same for their children.

Many fathers-to-be notice that their partners develop a nesting instinct when they become pregnant. They want a safe, secure place to have their baby. Security, in their minds, often equates with living in a house.

A Complicated and Expensive Decision

To buy a house, traditionally you first need to come up with a down payment, usually 10 to 20 percent of the purchase price of the home. This is not a hard and fast rule, of course, and mortgage brokers can structure different types of loans for you, depending on your income and resources. You need to be clear and careful about the terms and conditions of any deal you agree to or contract you sign. Basically, you need enough income or financial resources to qualify for a loan that will cover the balance of what you owe on the house. You need to take a hard look at what your monthly mortgage interest payments will be and how much overall debt you are taking on. And don't forget property taxes, household maintenance, and other expenses that will arise on top of your monthly mortgage payment. *The Everything®* *Homebuying Book, 3rd Edition,* is an excellent reference that provides information for buyers in a wide variety of situations.

ESSENTIAL

Generally, the financial burdens of raising children are most acute when the kids are in their younger years. As they grow older, some of these pressures ease. Your partner may also return to her job. Additionally, your income may grow over the years as your career develops. All of this will tend to give you more flexibility and the ability to take on more financial responsibility.

Balancing Your Priorities

To find an affordable place to buy, many families look for a home far away from where they work. While this may be a fiscally sound decision, it also increases their commute and keeps them away from their family longer during the day. Many fathers (and mothers) must get up early in the morning and leave for work before their children wake up. The only time they see them is in the evening.

A house is a worthwhile investment for both family and financial reasons, but once again, it's a matter of balancing your priorities. The increased financial demands of home ownership may force you and your partner to put your child in day care for much of the day. But you may feel this is worth it because you love your home and community and your child will be going to good schools and live in a neighborhood with lots of other kids around.

Life Insurance

Every man is different, but chances are you do not carry life insurance. After all, why should you? Until now it's just been you and your partner. You work, she works, and if something happened to you she has an income and she could take care of herself.

But this equation changes with the arrival of a baby. Now you have somebody else to think about: a tiny baby who depends on you for her care. What would happen to her if something bad happened to you?

Thoughts of Mortality

What a drag, right? Here you are, about to have a baby, one of the most life-affirming events in all of creation, and you've got to think about . . . your demise. This whole business of dying is only hypothetical, though, which is why some guys can't stand the idea of paying for life insurance: they feel like they're throwing money away.

That is certainly a truism about life insurance—you hope no one ever gets to collect on your policy. You never know what the future holds, though, and that's why you take out life insurance: because anything can happen.

Your Partner May Need Protection, Too

Money may be tight, and you may already be having a tough time paying the bills without forking over an annual life insurance premium, but you need to remember the situation you're in. Your baby is on her way, and your partner is about to take some time off work. She plans to return to her job as soon as she can, but perhaps only on a part-time basis at first because you both agree that she needs to devote as much time as possible to caring for the baby. That leaves you as the chief bread winner. Now, what if suddenly your income wasn't available?

If your partner draws an income, you need to think about getting some coverage for her, too. The theory behind life insurance is to help the survivors continue to live more or less as they have been, without being forced to move or suffer major disruptions because of financial hardship. This applies to women as well; if something happened to your partner, it might be tough for you alone to make up for the loss of income that would occur.

FACT

In most American households, both men and women earn incomes. Nevertheless, men are more likely to own life insurance than women. Probably because their incomes generally are higher, men also tend to carry more coverage. How much insurance you should carry is based on income and other factors. One rule of thumb is to carry enough life insurance so that if you pass on, your surviving spouse has the resources to pay off the mortgage.

Term Insurance Is the Way

Term insurance provides protection for a specific period of time (usually a year) and pays a benefit if you die during the term. You can purchase policies for terms of ten, fifteen, and twenty years, with premiums due each year. Your annual premiums—the amount you must pay to keep your coverage in effect—will stay the same throughout the life of the agreed-upon term.

Term insurance is superior to other forms of life insurance for young couples for a number of reasons. For one, it is less expensive. You can buy more coverage at a lower cost. The money you save can be used to cover your other bills, pay for a vacation, or invest in retirement or other long-term uses.

There is no cash value to a term insurance policy. However, because term is less expensive, agents make a smaller commission when they sell you a policy. Be aware of the motives of the insurance agent. She may try to steer you into other types of insurance because of the greater commission she will make from the sale.

Will and Estate Planning

Another thing that you and your partner need to do is prepare a will and do some estate planning. Your first question may be, "What estate?" Okay, so you're not Bill Gates, but you still own things—perhaps a house and a car or two—you have money in the bank (maybe), and then there's that antique pinball machine sitting in the garage that could command a hefty price on eBay.

You don't want to leave a big mess if something happens to you. You want your survivors to know what your wishes are for the things that are left behind, and nobody is going to know this unless you tell them.

QUESTION

Can I write a will without an attorney?
Yes, you can. Some states accept what is called a "holographic" or hand-written will. Write down your assets on a piece of paper, explain how you want them distributed in case of death, and sign and date it. Store the document in a safe place, and be sure to tell your partner about it.

With so many other things on your mind right now, this is definitely a long-range consideration, not something that needs to be addressed at this minute. At some point, though, you and your partner are going to need to sit down with an attorney who specializes in wills, trusts, and other estate planning issues to figure out all these matters. Online legal and financial services may also offer help in this regard; just make sure they are reliable before using them.

Saving for College

One of the most intimidating aspects of having children is the idea of paying for their future college education. The sums needed to go to college today, be it a private or public institution, are astronomical. Projections of what students will have to pay eighteen years from now—when your child will be an entering freshman—are even more daunting. Unless you have an oil field in your backyard, how can you expect to come up with that kind of dough?

If you are already thinking about saving and investing for college, you are to be commended for your foresight. Many fathers-to-be and fathers would prefer not to think about it at all. Paying for college is like climbing Mt. Everest: it's such a big and massive endeavor that you don't know where to start.

Virtually every year, college education costs increase far faster than the inflation rate. The annual costs for tuition, fees, room and board, books, travel, and incidental expenses for some public universities exceeds $25,000; for private institutions, the yearly cost can be much, much more. And one thing you can count on: as ridiculous as they are today, the costs will be higher still when your child is an incoming freshman.

Not only is investing for college intimidating, it's confusing as well. There are a seemingly endless array of savings plans and strategies and investment vehicles available to parents: section 529 savings plans, educational IRAs, custodial investment accounts, investment accounts set up in your name but earmarked for your child's education expenses, and so forth. Under certain restrictions and conditions, it is also possible to borrow against your 401(k) plan at work. You may also be able to borrow against your house. The list of expensive strategies goes on and on.

ESSENTIAL

Savings bonds to be used by your child for college make great gifts from grandparents, aunts, uncles, and others in the extended family. Although they may prefer to buy a toy or stuffed animal, you can gently suggest the idea of a savings bond as a gift for baby. It is truly a wonderful present for both children and their parents.

The decisions you make will likely have income tax implications, and this may in turn change what strategy you decide to pursue. How much you need to save depends on how old your child is and how great an investment window you have. Obviously, the amount you can put away depends greatly on how much you make, what your household expenses are, how you are set for retirement, and a zillion other factors.

It's best to start saving for college as early as possible, but there is no reason to freak about it now. You and your partner have enough on your mind without worrying about how to pay for Harvard. Setting aside even a small amount of money in a fund designated for your child's college education is a good start at this point.

Thinking about Retirement

Retirement is another of those down-the-road topics that may not feel immediately relevant to you. If you're in your twenties or early thirties, retirement may be something of an abstract issue to you. You figure you've still got plenty of time left to figure it out and put away what you need to make your golden years comfortable.

If you're in your late thirties or forties, however, the idea of retirement is starting to loom larger and larger. In twenty years or so you will be approaching sixty or sixty-five. At about the same time that you are beginning to head toward retirement, your child will be entering college. How are you going to pull both of those off at the same time?

Obviously the same basic rule applies here as in saving for college: get started as early as you can. Keep at it even if you are starting late and it doesn't seem like much. Having something set aside, no matter how little, is better than having nothing.

The best gift you can give your children when you are older is to have your financial act together. You and your partner want to be able to take care of yourselves, and this means having adequate resources in retirement. The last thing you want in your old age is to be a burden on your children. Getting a head start on planning and saving for these things will put you in a stronger position over the long run.

CHAPTER 9

Job, Work, Career

Becoming a father produces many changes in your life, but one thing will not change: your need to produce income to support yourself and your family. In this chapter you will learn how fatherhood can affect your job and career, how to approach your employer about taking time off when the baby comes, and other work-related issues.

Your Role as Provider

Much of the advice given to new fathers and fathers-to-be comes from females and has (naturally) a female point of view. It tends to focus on the nurturing aspects of a father's role: being an emotional support for your partner, being there for her during childbirth, assisting her around the house, and pitching in to help with the baby. These are important and useful tasks, but they do not encompass the entire universe of what a man needs to think about and do when he is about to become a father. A father's most fundamental job is to provide for his family.

The woman is in a vulnerable position during pregnancy. At some point as she nears full term, she will no longer be able to work at a job. After birth there will also be a time in which she cannot work and must tend to the baby's needs, as well as her own. As a father, you must help create a safe and protected place for the mother- and baby-to-be.

FACT

Be aware that your partner can receive paid medical disability benefits from her workplace for limited periods before and after birth. How much she receives depends on her salary, how long she has been on the job and paid into the system, and other factors. Laws vary from state to state, so do your homework. With her paid disability leave as well as perhaps her accrued paid vacation time and possibly paid personal and sick days, she can still have income when she is off work.

In the majority of families, the responsibility of being the primary income-earner still falls on the shoulders of the man, and most fathers are happy to have it. They see and know how much their partner is doing and they earnestly want to carry their share of the load. Contributing to their family by working at a job is a powerful way for them to do that.

Planning for When Baby Comes

When you have a baby, there are lots of variables to consider in terms of your work and your partner's work. One thing is certain: unless you are independently wealthy, you need to keep the dough rolling in. That means you need to keep your job or business going during the pregnancy and after the baby comes. That is, in a nutshell, the challenge of modern parenthood—balancing the needs of work and family.

Both fathers and mothers face this challenge together. While the man may make more money than his partner, that does not necessarily mean that his income alone can pay all the bills. The old paradigm—man as sole breadwinner, woman as homemaker—is becoming rarer and rarer in today's economic climate. The cost of living in some parts of the country is simply too high for families to make it on one income. Both Mom and Dad must work—at least one full-time and the other part-time, or both full-time.

Questions in Search of Answers

The most immediate impact on your financial situation is the temporary loss of your partner's income. She is going to have to take off from work in the eighth or ninth month—and if you are having twins or your partner is having a difficult pregnancy it may be much sooner than that. Then she will need to stay home with the baby for at least three weeks to a month, and preferably longer depending on her job situation and your finances.

Here is a question that needs an answer: how long does she want to stay home with the baby? Three months? Six months? Forever? You need to find out what her expectations are in this area because it will affect her job and your overall financial planning.

ESSENTIAL

Carve out some time with your partner to talk about these issues. You cannot decide them by yourself, nor should you. What your partner wants to do after the child is born will affect you, and vice versa. Talking about money with your partner is sometimes uncomfortable and emotional, but it is necessary.

Here is another question that needs an answer: how long do you want to take off from work after the baby is born? Due to the demands of the job and the need to keep money coming in, you will likely have less flexibility than your partner in this regard. If your job and finances permit it, you can easily stay home a week or so after the baby is born. After that you can play it by ear, maybe going back on a part-time basis the next week so you can still have lots of home time and help your partner with the baby. If you want to stay away from work longer, and some fathers do, you will obviously need to work it out with your employer and again, do some financial planning.

The Domino Effect

When it was just the two of you, you had more freedom on money issues. She made money and helped with the bills. But a baby in the house (or on the way) adds a new element to all financial and job-related decisions. Any action or decision by one member of the family will inevitably tip over a domino that affects the others.

Your partner, for instance, may want to quit her job after the baby comes. Or she may be willing to go back to work, but only after she has had plenty of time at home with her new child—say, a year. You may argue that you cannot afford for her to do that, but she may reply that raising a child is the most important thing in the world and her baby needs her.

Talk to your partner ahead of time. Get a sense of her wishes and expectations (although they are certainly subject to change). Well before the baby arrives, be prepared for the financial pressures that the three of you will face.

Steps to Take at Work

As was discussed in Chapter 2, every father-to-be must assess his company's work culture before he announces to his colleagues and his boss that he is going to become a father. Some companies will be supportive, but many will not because they believe becoming a father may make you slightly less devoted to the organization. You may be less willing (and able) to work after hours or travel for long periods away from home, and your boss may not like this.

In many cases, what happens when a man becomes a father is that he becomes more devoted to his job, not less. The reason is obvious: he needs that precious lucre. Many fathers-to-be work overtime (or take a second job) to pay off bills and build up their nest egg. Pregnancy is a good time for this because the baby has not yet arrived and your responsibilities at home are not as great as they will be after he's born.

Whatever your job, you are almost certainly not the first person in the history of your organization to become a parent. Your company (and your wife's, too) has policies and procedures in place regarding these issues. Here are the basic steps to take:

- Read the announcement postings in your lunchroom or break room to see what state and federal regulations apply to you.
- Learn about the Family Medical and Leave Act as well as the paid vacation, sick, and personal leave policies at your company.
- Talk to other employees who are parents to see how they proceeded.
- Review your employee manual (if your organization has one) to see what your rights and responsibilities are.
- Talk to the human resources department to make sure you understand the company's procedures and policies.
- Talk to your supervisor or boss about your plans.

The more informed you are, the better off you and your partner will be. Policies vary widely, though, and her company may handle things differently than yours does. She will need to go through the same information-gathering process at her job.

ALERT

Don't wait until the last minute to tell your employer that you are going to be a father and that you want some time off when the baby arrives. Most companies do not appreciate surprises of this kind. They need and deserve time to plan for your absence to ensure your work gets done while you're gone.

Family and Medical Leave Act

The Family and Medical Leave Act (FMLA) is a federal law that applies to private companies with fifty or more employees, government agencies, and public schools. Under its provisions, employees can take up to twelve weeks of unpaid leave for the birth and care of a child (and also for the arrival of adoptive or foster children). Although this leave must take place within a year of the birth, it need not be taken in consecutive weeks. The FMLA applies to both fathers and mothers, although they must have worked for the company for one year before the date of their leave.

The law states that when you return from work after an FMLA absence, you must have the same job you had before you left. You cannot be demoted or fired. Obviously, you must make sure your leave has received the organizational stamp of approval before you take off.

The FMLA applies to adoptive parents as well. Since your partner is not giving birth, however, she normally cannot receive disability leave or disability pay. After the baby comes, adoptive fathers and mothers may use the standard twelve weeks of unpaid leave, according to the FMLA guidelines, if they choose.

The Family and Medical Leave Act is a nice concept in principle, but because the leave is unpaid, many couples do not use it. They cannot afford to take that much time off without income. Men who work in the private sector need to be particularly careful because their employer may look askance at them if they ask for too much time off. In fact, some employers disapprove of men taking any time off when their baby arrives. They feel that it is not necessary, and that men need to stay on the job.

Other Strategies

Some companies offer paternity leave to new fathers, similar to the Family and Medical Leave Act. Like FMLA, paternity leave is almost always unpaid, making it a hollow benefit. Some family men cannot afford to go without a paycheck for even a week.

FACT

There is a link between how much time a man spends with his family and how much money he earns. One sampling of fathers showed that for every additional $10,000 a man earns, he spends an average of five minutes a day less with his children during the week.

If you are a father-to-be who wants to take time off to be with your new-born child, it is realistic to expect that you will likely have to use your paid vacation leave. You can start saving your days as soon as you know the baby is coming. Just don't pile up more days than allowed; some companies will let their employees accrue only a set amount of vacation time before they must use it. As a parent, you should always keep a few paid vacation days in reserve as you may need one to take your child to a doctor's appointment or attend to some other unexpected family matter.

Another possibility is paid sick or personal leave. Some companies, however, will not let their employees use sick time unless they are actually ill. Others allow the use of sick or personal leave if the time off is considered part of the time taken under the FMLA. Again, policies vary, so talk to your company about how it handles this issue.

Negotiating Time and Flexibility

If you're like most new fathers, you will want to take off at least one week after the baby arrives. When he was prime minister of Great Britain some years ago, Tony Blair created a political firestorm when he announced that he wasn't going to take any time off from his job when his child was born. Critics lambasted him for advocating a pro-father, pro-family line and yet not practicing it himself. Blair then caved in and spent the week at home with his wife changing their newborn's poopy diapers.

One week is certainly a reasonable request, but what about two? Again, if your employer approves, and assuming you can afford it, there is no reason why you can't request a longer stay at home if you're interested. At the end of two weeks, you will almost certainly have had your fill of full-time baby craziness and be anxious to get back to the relative sanity of work.

Of course, you do not want to make any requests that threaten your job security, nor do you want to inconvenience your employer too much. Remember you are looking for flexibility, not a whole bunch of time off. Flexibility is the most important thing you can negotiate for yourself at work.

Why Flexibility?

Flexibility at work means everything when you have a family. If your partner is at home and not working at a job, you can rely on her to do much of what needs to be done with the baby (at least when you're at work). But when your partner goes back to her job, all bets are off. You're going to have to step in and help out, and for that you will need flexibility.

The baby needs to go to the doctor. You have to drop her off at day care or pick her up. There is an emergency. Your partner has a late meeting and needs you to get the baby. Because of all this and more, having a small child constantly demands your time and energy.

Negotiating Flexibility

Whether or not you can get much flexibility at work depends on lots of factors. First comes your employer and the nature of your work. It may be that your company absolutely needs you to be on the job from eight to five, and there's nothing you can do about it. Other companies may be willing to be more flexible on hours as long as the work still gets done. In that case, perhaps you can do some of your work at home.

ALERT

Your boss or employer must follow company policies. He cannot grant special privileges to you without having his other employees notice and perhaps complain and ask for special favors themselves. That is why it sometimes helps to scout things out—talk to other employees, know what has been done in the past—before approaching him.

Here is where being a good employee pays off. If you are a conscientious worker who has paid his dues at the company, flexibility will be easier to negotiate than if you have been perceived as demanding or negative in the past. Whatever plan you come up with to create flexibility, remember that your boss is not going to be thinking first about you but about his own situation. You must devise a plan that works for him too, or it's not going to fly.

Small Ways to Gain Flexibility

For many fathers and fathers-to-be, flexibility on the job is a luxury. They may work for a business that cannot or will not grant privileges to its employees. They may run a small business with only a few employees and simply need to be there from sun up to sun down. Or they may work for themselves and shutting down the business, even for a little while, means the money stops coming in.

Still, even guys with the tightest schedules imaginable can usually find ways to create some flexibility that allows them to spend more time with their family. Perhaps you can juggle your hours a little—say, come in at seven and leave at four. This gets you home earlier in the evening, which corresponds better with the baby's schedule and allows you to spend more time with her. Another way to create time is to take a shorter lunch break, which may enable you to leave work earlier.

Other Job Options

Everybody's work situation is different, so finding flexibility will require different solutions for different people. You and your employer may be able to agree on a more radical approach, such as squeezing your regular forty-hour week into four days, rather than the usual five. This alternative work schedule, in which you power through four consecutive ten-hour days so that you have three full days off, is becoming more commonplace.

These approaches may only be practical for a short time. Eventually, your employer may need you to work your regular hours, as you always have. Until that happens, though, you have managed to get some extra time to spend at home with your newborn. Here are some other job options worth thinking about and possibly discussing with your employer (although they will usually result in reduced pay, which may not be possible or acceptable to you):

- *Job sharing*—dividing your duties and hours with another person to give you more free time.
- *Part-time*—reducing your regular hours on the job.

- *Voluntary reduced work time*—taking a cut in pay in exchange for one afternoon a week off.
- *Telecommuting*—working from home a day or two a week.
- *Sabbatical*—taking an extended leave from the company.

If you are like most men, you are not able or willing to take a cut in pay or to reduce your income, even if you want to stay home more with your child. With your partner not producing income for the moment, you need to work. In essence, when you have a baby, you automatically take on a second full-time job—fatherhood.

Daddy Track and Mommy Track Concerns

The concept of a "Mommy Track" has received quite a bit of attention over the years. The term refers to mothers who are placed by their employer in a different, and lesser, category than other women and men who do not have similar family demands vying for their time. Some believe that women on the Mommy Track receive lower pay and are less likely to be promoted at work. If so, this hurts both men and women because it affects the entire family's income and its prospects for the future.

Many fathers face a similar situation. They are put on a Daddy Track and regarded in a different light than other men, usually single, who are willing to devote long, long hours to the success of the organization. This is usually not overt and nothing is said openly. Still, many new fathers feel these pressures and are not sure what to do about them.

FACT

Earning a living is important to men. So is being able to spend time with their families. Polls consistently show that a vast majority of men prefer a work schedule that gives them time with their family. They would rather make a little less and spend more time at home than earn a high salary that requires them to be away a great deal.

Your Changing View of Work

The Daddy Track is a kind of glass ceiling for men. If you are perceived as something less than 100 percent devoted to the company, you are going to rise only so high in the ranks. After that, you will find that your head starts bumping against something that you cannot see but that is as hard as a rock. Men who work in sales jobs that require lots of travel are susceptible to being labeled as Daddy Trackers because they no longer wish to be gone so long from home.

Looked at from the employer's point of view, however, you can almost argue that the Daddy Track makes sense on some level. When you become a father, your values do change. You are not committed to work in quite the same way that you were before and you may not wish to put in the same hours you did in the past because you want to go home to be with your family. In short, your company's goals may no longer correspond with your own.

More Motivation to Work

Some employers do not place new fathers on a Daddy Track, and there are good reasons for this. They realize that new fathers are among the most motivated of their employees. New fathers suddenly have another mouth to feed in the family, and they know they had better keep their jobs.

Francis Ford Coppola, the director of *The Godfather* and many other movies, has talked about the trend nowadays for men to put off fatherhood until later and later in their life. Their thinking is that they want to establish themselves in their career before a baby comes along. Coppola, who is a father and grandfather, believes this attitude is backward. He feels that having a baby can serve as supreme motivation for a young man. You cannot screw around any longer in your career because you've got a little creature who is counting on you.

Moving into the Future

Many fathers avoid being put on a Daddy Track by going along with their company's program as a means of getting ahead in their career. In this way, they feel, they can make money and best help their family. Although their job may not give them as much time with their kids as they'd like, they swallow their regrets and move ahead. This way of doing things, however, may not work for you.

Ultimately, if you work for a company or organization that does not support your desire to be involved with your family, you may have to find a new job. It is as simple—or as hard—as that. Your life has changed, and your job and your lifestyle may no longer be a good fit.

Another thing you may realize—and you may have figured this out early in the pregnancy—is that your current job is not cutting it. The hours may be fine and the employer may be as flexible as a rubber band, but it just doesn't pay enough. At some point, you may have to start looking around for a new position or go back to school for more education that will help get you a better job with higher pay.

Getting a Better Job

With your personal life heading into uncertain, perhaps rocky seas, it is best to stay steady and solid in your work life. You obviously do not want to do anything that will put your job—and your health insurance coverage—at risk at this time.

But in some situations, pregnancy may be the prompt you need to make a change in your employment situation. A baby can change your attitude toward your job or work. What may have been a perfect fit before may not be quite so ideal anymore.

Reasons for Dissatisfaction

Due to the increased financial pressures on you, the money you're making at your job may no longer cut it. Now that you have a baby at home, that two-hour commute to and from work may seem impossible. You want to get home at a decent hour so you can do more with your boy than give him a kiss at night before he goes to bed, not spend your time sitting in traffic.

Before the baby you may have worked regularly till six or seven at night. After the baby comes, you'll probably find yourself slipping out of the office a few minutes before five, and your supervisor may not like this. She may have come to expect long hours from you, and she's disappointed now that you seem to have developed split loyalties between the company and your family. This may cause her to give you a hard time, which makes you think about making a change.

ALERT

You may be dissatisfied with your job. It may not pay enough or offer adequate flexibility. Even so, it's worth underlining the point: do not make any rash moves. You need to hang on to your job until after the child is born and probably for some months after that. It provides needed income and maybe your family's health and hospitalization coverage as well.

The Need for More Education

In order to support their families and give them a better life, many fathers realize that they need to get more training or go back to school. It is possible you will find yourself in this situation. In today's rapidly changing (and sometimes precarious) economy, it is no exaggeration to say that the job you hold at this moment may not exist in five or ten years.

The bright side of this picture is that the changes occurring in the economy are also creating jobs and opportunities that did not exist five or ten years ago. To take advantage of these opportunities, you may need to get a specific kind of training or a more advanced college degree. You may need to quit your job or reduce your hours and take out loans and obtain financial assistance.

Obviously you will need to work all this out beforehand with your partner. If you're earning less money, she will likely have to take up the slack with her income. You may want to wait until the baby is a little older before making any radical changes. But these are the kinds of changes—leaving a job in order to go back to school to get a better job—that develop momentum when you start a family.

Working at Home

An increasing number of men today are self-employed (or work some hours for their employer at home). You may be one of them, working in your spare bedroom at home, sitting in front of the computer in your bathrobe and slippers, and setting your own hours and schedule depending on the work. Because of this, you may not have to worry about pleasing a boss or adjusting your schedule to fit someone else.

In any case, your home office is about to be thrown into complete turmoil. Quiet and sanity and free time will all be relics of the past. Why is that, you ask? Because in the space of a few short weeks or months, you are about to be invaded.

Home Invasion

In the last weeks of her pregnancy, your partner will probably stop working. Consequently, she will spend more time at home than she has in the past. This will represent a change for you because you are used to working alone and having the place to yourself during the day, but you will adjust. This adjustment is nothing, though, compared to the one you must make when the baby appears.

A baby does not just arrive in a house—she takes over. Her needs reign supreme, and they must be satisfied instantly or tears will stream down her cute chubby cheeks and her cries will ring out like a fire engine siren. Even when her needs are filled, she still cries. As her father, there is nothing for you to do but feed her and change her and walk her and burp her and pray that she falls asleep at some point to give you a break.

Finding a Quiet Space Outside the Home

But you still have to work, right? Even if you keep the door to your office closed at all times—heck, even if you soundproof the door and the walls—it is going to be a challenging work environment. You will hear the baby's cries, as well as the tired desperation in your partner's voice, and inevitably you will open the door and offer to help. Your partner may not wait for you to offer—she may pound on the door and demand it. In any event, when you work at home with a new baby, expect to help out. A lot.

During the pregnancy, it might be wise to check out other possible workplace options than your own home. Can you do some of your work at a library? What about temporarily borrowing or renting a room at a friend's or neighbor's house? If these are not practical, you may want to investigate the possibility of renting an office for six months to a year to get a quiet space to work.

You can also anticipate that you will be working unusual hours in the first months after the baby comes home. You will need to take care of the baby to give your partner a break and let her sleep, and your partner will need to watch her while you work and sleep.

Flexibility is the key when you have a child, whether you work at home, at a job, or whether you run your own business. Advance planning is also useful. Take the steps you need to take at work to find out how much paid leave you and your wife can take. Talk to your employer, who may be sympathetic to you and willing to arrange a schedule that works for you both. Thinking ahead will help you get the flexibility you need.

CHAPTER 10

Health: Yours, Hers, and the Baby's

Your number-one concern as a father is the health and well-being of your partner and the child on the way. But while you, and the doctors and, everyone else are paying so much attention to them, don't forget another important person: yourself. Here are some tips on keeping a sound body—and mind—during pregnancy.

Leading the Way

One issue that occasionally pops up in sports today is whether or not professional athletes are role models. Former basketball great and NBA analyst Charles Barkley doesn't think so. "I ain't no role model," he said once. "If kids are looking up to me to be their role model, they're looking in the wrong place. Their mommy and daddy—that's who their role models are."

Whether you think pro athletes are role models or not, Barkley definitely has got it right. A child's most influential role models are his father and mother. Babies and children are like little sponges, mimicking the habits and behavior of the people who are around them the most. A child first learns from his parents, siblings, and extended family, while the other influences on his life—television, school, peers—come later.

This realization will hit home to you most powerfully at some point after the baby is born. He will be putting up a squawk about something—it's always something—and you will hear a familiar inflection in his voice. Or he will crinkle his nose, or move his hands in a certain way, and you will think, "Hey, that's me. That is what I do." You were not consciously teaching him how to do this, and yet he picked it up by watching you and being around you.

Alcohol

The realization that you can have such a profound impact on another human being can be humbling for many men. It is one reason why some have trouble making the adjustment to fatherhood. "Hey, I can barely take care of myself," they say to themselves, "and now I'm supposed to take care of a kid? I don't think so."

Although your partner is a mature adult, capable of acting and making decisions on her own, what you do can have a big impact on her too. You are not her role model in the same way that you will be for your child, but your behavior can influence hers in both negative and positive ways.

You may be thinking, "Okay, so my partner has to quit drinking because she is pregnant, what does this have to do with me?" Common sense will tell you that if you're tossing down Grey Goose martinis night after night, it is going to be harder for your partner to stay away from the alcohol. There will be more liquor around the house, and that means there is more temptation for her to pour herself a glass of something when she's feeling down.

QUOTE

As you read this chapter, Kathleen Sauter, a mother of three, wants both Dads and Moms to remember that eventually the pregnancy will end and you will have a baby, and then you can go back to having a drink now and then (assuming you drink). "Store up plenty of wine for the future," Sauter says, laughing. "That's my baby survival tip. Because after baby comes you're going to need a nice, relaxing drink now and then."

Different couples work it out in different ways. One mother-to-be was concerned about her partner's heavy drinking and wanted him to stop, but he refused. One night they went out together, and when he ordered his usual—double Scotch on the rocks and a beer—she did the same. When he drank his, she drank hers.

"If you insist on getting drunk again," she told him, "so am I." And even though she was five months pregnant, she meant it. His drinking, if he kept at it, was potentially going to harm their child and destroy their relationship. He got the message, and it scared him to death. Eventually he gave up drinking—not just during the pregnancy, but for good.

Cigarette Smoking

Smoking cigarettes is one of the worst health hazards of pregnancy. Pregnant women are urged to stop because the smoke they inhale does not just go into their lungs—the baby gets an unhealthy dose of it too. Smoking by Mom can cause mammoth problems for the child, such as developmental disabilities and disorders, pregnancy complications, premature birth, and even death.

That's the bad news, but there is good news. Evidence to date shows that even if a woman has smoked all her life, as long as she does not do so during pregnancy, her child will not be harmed. A mother-to-be needs to put away the cigarettes as soon as she learns that she's pregnant.

Finding the Motivation

Mark Twain said that quitting smoking was the easiest thing in the world; he had done it thirty or forty times. Most smokers would heartily agree. People may know intellectually that it is bad for them and they need to quit, but how do you actually do it?

Under ordinary circumstances, it is hard sometimes to find the motivation to stop smoking (or drinking alcohol). But when you are about to become a parent, motivation is no longer in short supply. You know what you need to do and why, and suddenly it no longer seems impossible.

Once More, with Feeling

If your partner smokes and is pregnant, it is best for her to stop smoking. She may be the most motivated and determined person in the world, but quitting anything cold turkey is hard for anyone. Once again, she is going to need your help.

If you smoke, it is going to make it that much harder for her to quit or cut back because she will want to light up when she sees you smoking. Then there is the issue of secondhand smoke. Having your pregnant partner breathing the smoke from your cigarettes may harm the life inside her. Even if you take it outside or try not to do it in her presence, she is still going to smell it on your breath and clothes.

ALERT

Nobody's perfect. If your partner, in a moment of weakness, breaks down and has a cigarette, it is not the end of the world. Just encourage her to stop at one and get back on her healthful track. A forgiving approach will reap far better results than a critical or judgmental one.

As with the restrictions on drinking, you may view this as punitive: "She's the one who's pregnant. Why do I have to suffer too?" Another way to look at it is that quitting is something the two of you can do together. While she's pregnant, make a pact and agree to throw away the cigarettes and keep them out of the house. Doing it as a couple—with each person trying not to disappoint the other—may give you further motivation and determination.

Recreational and Over-the-Counter Drugs

Recreational drugs—such as marijuana, cocaine, or LSD—fall into the same category as cigarettes and alcohol; they are bad news. They can do damage to the baby in the womb, producing birth defects and other maladies that can affect her for her entire life.

Some people would argue that marijuana should not be lumped with cocaine and other illegal drugs, saying that it is less harmful and more benign to its users. As with cigarettes, past marijuana use does not evidently affect a developing fetus. But, again, like cigarettes, smoking pot while pregnant is a different story. The smoke your partner inhales affects the placenta, which serves as the baby's protective cocoon. Marijuana should be avoided during pregnancy just like any other drug.

ESSENTIAL

One of the great things about having a child is that you do not think just in terms of yourself. You recognize that your actions will influence your partner today and your baby tomorrow. Your willingness to clean up some of your old habits, if they need cleaning up, will be viewed positively by your partner as another sign of support for her.

Your partner needs to speak to her doctor about any over-the-counter drugs or antibiotics she is currently taking or plans to take. Any kind of over-the-counter medication, even aspirin, may have harmful side effects on the baby. In matters of health, when you are dealing with pregnancy, follow a simple rule: err on the side of caution. Be aware of the possible risks of any drug before taking it.

Hot Tubs and Environmental Concerns

Other potential health concerns for your partner are hot tubs. She should avoid tubbing or even taking hot baths while she is pregnant because excessive heat can harm the baby. She should not get too hot, or exhausted, during exercise for the same reason. During flu season, she should talk to her doctor before receiving a flu vaccination to see if it is advisable for her.

Environmental issues can also affect pregnant women. If it's a bad smog day with poor air quality, it might be advisable for her to skip her afternoon walk. It is also best for her to avoid lawn and garden pesticides. If you have a pet, you need to clean the litter box and handle the poop with gloves, not her. Household cleaning products can also produce fumes that make her queasy. Microwaves are considered to be safe for pregnant women to use, although the food should not be placed in plastic wrap.

With a baby on the way, couples often get into home improvement. Chapter 13 discusses this in greater depth, but since this is usually the guy's job, you need to be aware of the dust you're stirring up and the products you're working with when you turn that spare bedroom into a nursery. Chemicals in new carpet, paint, insulation, and other building materials can be released into the air through evaporation, or "outgassing." Use paint that is free of lead and other potentially toxic substances. Remodeling an old house can loosen dust, paint chips, and asbestos into the air, and this may also affect her.

Eating Healthy

Quit drinking. Stop smoking. Cut out the illegal drugs. No more hot tub parties, at least for a while. You might perceive all of these as negatives in that you must cease and desist from activities that you were doing before your partner became pregnant and that you both considered, well, fun. For you to quit doing these things requires sacrifice. Unfortunately, there is no getting around this.

Less of a negative and more of a positive is the idea of eating healthy. Unless you're a junk food junkie, this requires less sacrifice. For your pregnant partner and that baby *in utero*, the benefits of a nutrition-packed diet are profound. Hey, it might even pay dividends for dear old Dad, too.

Foods to Avoid

Okay, so it's not all positive and some sacrifice is required in this department, too. There are some foods your pregnant partner needs to avoid. The two of you are going to have to stay away from your favorite sushi place for a while, because raw fish is forbidden. So are any dishes featuring raw meat—such as steak tartare—or uncooked eggs. Your partner should drink only pasteurized milk.

All fish, meat, chicken, pork, and eggs need to be cooked thoroughly because cooking eliminates those nasty bacteria and parasites that can increase the risk of infection or harmful disease. If you're on kitchen duty, and you chopped up the chicken or fish for dinner, make sure to clean the knife and the cutting board before using them again to chop the veggies.

Coffee and Tea

You can breathe a sigh of relief on this one. Your partner (and by association, you) is not going to be asked to give up her morning Starbucks. Coffee and tea with caffeine are relatively benign in their effects and have not yet been placed by medical authorities on the banned substances list. There is a difference between heavy and light caffeine consumption, though, and your partner needs to practice moderation. She may want to switch to decaffeinated coffee or herbal teas during this period.

FACT

Studies indicate that it appears to be safe for a pregnant woman to drink as much as one twelve-ounce cup of caffeinated coffee a day. Keep in mind, though, that the higher the consumption of caffeine, the greater the risk of a miscarriage. The chance of a miscarriage increases for pregnant women who drink more than the twelve-ounce standard.

Remember that some soft drinks, chocolate, and other substances contain caffeine. Too much caffeine can affect a person's mood and may make your partner's emotional ups and downs even more pronounced than they already are. If she's on a coffee high, she may push herself when what her body really needs is rest. Also, drinking a rich, coffee-house brew may give her an artificial feeling of fullness, causing her not to eat more wholesome foods.

Developing Healthy Habits

By now, you have noticed a clear trend in this whole pregnancy deal—the burden of just about everything falls more heavily on the woman. She is the one who must quit smoking, cut back on the drinking, not take cough syrup without first calling the doctor, and stop guzzling those mocha frappucinos.

And you? Well, your participation in her abstinence is optional. You have the freedom to decide whether to go along with all of this for the simple reason that your choices do not matter as much to the baby's health. You could drink like a fish and smoke unfiltered cigarettes until your lungs collapsed, and still you would not directly affect the baby.

QUESTION

What if I feel intimidated by the pregnancy?
Many men do. Partly this is because they have never experienced anything like this before and they know nothing about it. Of course, your partner didn't know anything either until she got pregnant. The more involved you become, the less intimidated you will feel.

However, you can choose to acknowledge that what you do does make a difference. You can definitely make a positive contribution to your partner's pregnancy and the developing life of your child through the choices you make. Your support and encouragement will help her make these sometimes hard sacrifices. Besides what has already been discussed in this chapter, here are some things she needs to do and that you can help her with:

- Take her pregnancy vitamins every day
- Drink lots of fluids
- Drink milk, or eat other calcium-rich foods such as yogurt or cottage cheese
- Eat a variety of fruits, vegetables, and whole-grain foods
- Get plenty of protein in her diet
- Cut down on her fat intake
- Exercise lightly on a regular basis
- Get plenty of rest

Your partner has likely figured out much of this already. If she is like many first-time moms, she been reading the pregnancy books like crazy and talking to her doctor and everybody else who has been through it to learn all she can. Still, your active, engaged presence in what she is going through will be a boon to her and help you feel more connected to your child in the end.

Cooking

Every couple has their own kitchen culture. With some couples, the man does most of the cooking while in others, the man and the woman share the job. Some couples work it out along more traditional lines, with the woman doing most of the cooking.

Almost invariably, the man must take a more assertive role in the food preparation and shopping when a woman becomes pregnant. Particularly early in the pregnancy, when the woman is suffering from morning sickness, she may not feel like cooking or eating anything. If a guy wants something to eat, he is probably going to have to fix it himself.

The Joy of Cooking

Men who are used to having their partners cook for them may resent this change of roles. They may prefer the old system—she cooks, he washes the dishes—and decide to simply make do as best they can until their partner feels good enough to get back into the kitchen again.

For other fathers-to-be, pregnancy may present them with an unexpected opportunity. Suddenly thrust into the kitchen, they may find they actually like cooking and get into it.

QUOTE

"I love to cook, but when I was pregnant, there were some nights I was so tired I couldn't even face the kitchen," says Jennifer Kaiser, mother of four and wife of this book's author, Kevin Nelson. "Your partner will surely feel like that some nights too. Step in, ask her what she feels like eating (if anything), and fix it for her. It doesn't have to be a culinary masterpiece. But believe me, she will appreciate it."

Stick to the Basics

The first thing to know about cooking, if you are a novice, is that you do not need to be Bobby Flay or Mario Batali to impress your partner. You may remember from your bachelor days that a woman will appreciate almost anything you prepare because it means she doesn't have to make a meal herself. It shows you are trying, and your pregnant partner may appreciate this most of all.

One wonderful element of good cooking is using fresh ingredients. Whatever meal you choose to make—roast chicken with green beans, spaghetti and meatballs with a tossed green salad, chicken burritos and guacamole dip—will taste better if you avoid frozen or canned vegetables and rely on fresh produce. Green leafy vegetables and fruits are a rich source of vitamin C, iron, calcium, and other good minerals, all of which your partner needs (as do you).

Consult a Cookbook

The joke about men is that when driving a car, they refuse to ask for directions. They would rather drive around in circles than stoop to the indignity of asking a stranger to straighten them out. This may be true of some guys in the kitchen as well. They regard cookbooks much the way Blutarski in *Animal House* looked askance at textbooks and refused to open one.

ALERT

When cooking for a pregnant woman, you may need to go easy on spicy or hot foods. More exotic cuisines such as East Indian, Thai, or barbecue may not sit well in her stomach. Red wine can often transform a routine meal into something special, but it is best to keep it in the cabinet during the pregnancy.

Cookbooks contain recipes and show basic techniques. They tell you how long your pot roast should stay in the oven and at what temperature. Cooking magazines and loads of websites also feature recipes and cooking tips, some of which are targeted to men.

Exercise

The benefits of exercise for pregnant women are as clear and strong as the benefits of eating well. Exercise can help her stand up straighter, improve her blood circulation, give her a better night's sleep, give her a boost in energy, and possibly relieve constipation. Exercise can give her a mental break too, taking her mind off the pregnancy for a while.

The need for your partner to engage in moderate exercise may produce an unintended benefit for you as well. You may be willing to put down the remote, get off the couch, and take a walk or bicycle ride with her. While she gains pounds, you may be inspired to lose a few.

ESSENTIAL

Your partner needs to speak to her obstetrician before she starts exercising. Skiing, horseback riding, and other high-impact sports in which she could potentially fall and hurt herself and the baby are off-limits. Nor can she lift weights or relax after her exertion in a hot tub. Her doctor will be able to give her guidelines on safe activities.

Now you may not be a couch potato. On the contrary, you may be a total gym rat, a triathlete, or the guy at the Y who takes on all comers and kicks butt at the Saturday one-on-one basketball games. Your first thought may be, "Me? Exercise with a pregnant woman? You gotta be kidding."

Like so many of the other activities discussed in this chapter, your partner will be more inclined to exercise if you go with her. The downside for you is that you may have to slow down a little (or a lot) due to her condition. Here are a few suggestions on what you can do together:

- Walking or light jogging
- Bicycling
- Swimming
- Ping pong or paddle tennis
- Friendly game of tennis
- Badminton
- Golf (probably with a cart)
- Light yoga or stretching

Exercise will help your partner feel and look better, and it will be equally beneficial for you. You'll get these benefits at the same time that you and your partner are engaged in a shared activity, thus promoting togetherness as a couple. Regular moderate exercise may promote another aspect of your life as well—your sex life.

Her Need for Rest

Virtually from the beginning of her pregnancy, your partner has been tired. More tired than you have ever seen her before. So tired, in fact, that she almost seems like a different person. Even on her good days, she seems to have little energy.

This affects everything. You ask her to go on a walk with you, but she doesn't feel up to it. You put on your chef's hat and whip up a masterpiece in the kitchen, but she is too tired (or sick) to eat much of it. Worse still, she never feels like going out anymore. Most nights, all she wants to do is sleep.

Such is life with a pregnant woman. She may have periods of high energy—particularly in the second trimester—but even then she complains frequently about how tired she is. Her tiredness may be a constant of her pregnancy—and a bit of a drag from your point of view.

It is essential to realize, though, that rest is critical for her. The old saying goes, "A pregnant woman is no longer eating for one, but for two," and this seems equally true in the sleep department. She is sleeping for herself as well as for that life growing inside her.

CHAPTER 11

Sex During Pregnancy

Sex during pregnancy is not one of those oxymorons like "jumbo shrimp," "working vacation," or "black light." Sex during pregnancy does indeed exist, and many couples report that it can be quite rewarding. This chapter explains how to get the most from your sex life while moving toward greater intimacy with your partner.

Sex and the Pregnant Father

Pregnancy marks a new phase in your sexual relationship with your partner. The two of you are in the process of producing a child—another human being in the making. This simple yet breathtaking development has triggered a series of changes in your life, including your sex life.

When you were single, your sex life may have been an active one. You may have dated a variety of women and had longer relationships with some of them. Or maybe you dated only a select few. Out of all your prior experiences came the luckiest one: your partner, the mother of your child.

QUOTE

"As strange as it might seem at first," says Kevin Nelson, father of four and author of this book, "pregnancy can actually be a pretty good time for sex for both you and your partner. There are things you have to work through, of course. But since she already is pregnant, she can't get pregnant again, right? It's a surprisingly liberating feeling."

When you went from being strictly single to a man in a committed relationship, your sex life inevitably changed. In the beginning, the infatuation you felt for your partner produced frequent sparks in the bedroom. Over the years you may have found that these sparks, while still white-hot in intensity, occur less frequently. Every couple's sexual relationship changes and becomes different as their feelings for each other mature.

Now you are entering a period of uncertainty and perhaps even confusion. Your partner's body is changing along with, perhaps, her libido. You're not sure what it all means—for now or in the future. You have had to grow and adjust to changing circumstances in every phase in your past sex life, and this one is no different.

Understanding Your Partner

It is worthwhile to note that your partner is likely to be experiencing many of the same emotions that you are—perhaps to an even greater degree. She has never been through any of this before, either. The physical and emotional changes she is experiencing, while giving her immense joy on one level, may fill her with doubts. She may also wonder what all of this means to the two of you as a couple.

She may worry about your feelings for her at this time. Do you still find her attractive? Does she still turn you on?

What Stage Is She In?

The key to sex during pregnancy is understanding the stage your partner is in and adjusting to it. Because your partner may frequently feel nauseated and tired thanks to the morning sickness the first trimester brings, her desire for sex may be somewhat limited. Your partner's body grows to its biggest proportions in the last trimester, and feeling heavy and (as always) tired she may not exactly feel like a sex kitten at this time either.

FACT

One study found that after about the third month, 10 percent of all pregnant couples were not having sex. By the ninth month, the number of abstaining couples had risen to 33 percent. However, in this same study, about 40 percent of all the couples surveyed were still having and enjoying sex into the ninth month.

Every woman and every woman's pregnancy are different. But, generally speaking, the best time for sexual relations for pregnant couples is in the second trimester—from months four to six. Your partner's morning sickness has passed, and yet her body has not gotten ungainly. Her hormones may have imbued her with that famous pregnancy "glow" when everything about her radiates with she-wolf energy. These surging feelings of health and wellness may translate into a renewed interest in bedroom activities.

Tuning into Her

A man's body is, in the sexual sphere, obviously far different from a woman's. Men do not menstruate, and their moods do not rise and fall during the month because of this. Though a woman stops menstruating during pregnancy, her moods are still connected to the rhythms of her body.

Don't take it personally if your partner seems uninterested in sex. It is not because she suddenly finds you less attractive or somehow less of a man. Don't blame her, either. Her feelings about sex are being shaped to a large degree by the hormonal changes occurring inside her body.

Because of the physical changes she is experiencing, her libido may have decreased. She may simply not be as interested in sex as she was before. It's nobody's fault; it's just the way it is. Then again, there may be instances in the second trimester or at other times during the pregnancy when she is just as horny for you as she was when you first started sleeping together. It is up to you to assess her mood in terms of sex and act accordingly.

Your Attitude

When they offer suggestions about sex, most pregnancy manuals advise men to tune into what their partners are feeling and to be sensitive to her moods and her situation at that moment. This is good advice, but what these manuals never seem to acknowledge is that the man may be experiencing a variety of feelings, too.

Many men get turned on by pregnancy and their partner's pregnant body. They see creating a child is a happy affirmation of their masculinity. Other men are not so sure about the whole business. Their feelings are more complicated, perhaps even troubled to some extent. These feelings may affect their view of sex during pregnancy and their relationship with their partner.

Your View of Her Body

It's okay to admit it (at least to yourself): you may not be entirely sold on what your partner looks like at this moment. This may have temporarily decreased your desire for her. A tiny voice in the back of your head may be wondering if this is going to turn into a permanent condition—you less interested in her sexually, and she less interested in you.

Some fathers-to-be, however, do not mind the extra weight on their partners; they dig it, in fact. As a pregnant woman gets closer to delivering, her breasts begin to lactate. The father-to-be can taste the sweetness of mother's milk even before his child does.

Attitude is everything. If you are put off initially by your partner's changing body shape, try to take a different attitude about it. Relax. Accept it for what it is, and know that it is temporary. If she senses you being distant or critical, she may in turn withdraw from you physically, and this will affect your togetherness as a couple.

Your Partner as Mom

Your partner may be thrilled at the prospect of becoming a mother. However, your view of this new development may be somewhat different. While you may know that your partner is going to be a sensational parent, she is nevertheless taking on a new role. No longer merely your partner, she is becoming your child's mother as well.

Sexually speaking, this may give you pause. You've never made love to somebody's mother before, certainly not the mother of your own child. A thought like that can get into your head and play games with sexual desire, but only if you let it.

QUESTION

How do you approach your partner for sex during this time?
Ask her. Talk to her. She may be grateful for the chance to confide what she is feeling. Your openness to her may lead her to feel more open to you and a warmer, more relaxed atmosphere for you both.

Your feelings about your partner may be complicated by your feelings about your own mother and her relationship with your father. Your father may have been an outsider in his own home, a guy who could often be found out in the garage because that was where he was most comfortable. Perhaps this was partly his own predilection, but it could also have been the result of your mother's shutting him out of the life of the family. Could this happen to you too?

Trust in Time

Some of the changes you are experiencing with your partner may, in fact, be more or less permanent. After she gives birth, she may not lose all of the weight she gained during the pregnancy. Even if she loses the weight, chances are that her shape, particularly her breasts and hips, will be different. You may have no other choice but to learn to live with the new contours of her body.

It will take time for the great physical thing the two of you had before pregnancy to return. It often takes months before the two of you can comfortably have sex again, partly because her body will need to physically heal after giving birth. Even when it becomes physically okay for her, her mind may be on the baby and her own issues and not on you. You may not receive much satisfaction. Beyond that, you may wonder if she isn't into sex anymore for some reason that has to do with you.

But things could go the other way, too. She may lose a few pounds. Her sexual desire (as well as yours) may return to normal. What you two had together in the bedroom may come back better than before. All of these things can happen, but they will take time.

Will Sex Hurt the Baby?

This is often one of the first concerns of both men and women after they learn they are pregnant. Will sex hurt the baby, possibly causing a miscarriage or other problems? In almost every case, in a normal pregnancy, the answer is no. Both the man and woman can feel relaxed about having sex. It will not affect the child, who is well protected inside the womb.

Doctors and other experts on pregnancy encourage couples to continue having normal sexual relations, if they feel up to it. You may be parents-to-be now, but you are still a functioning couple. A vital aspect of a good relationship is healthy sexual relations. Although your partner's sex drive will go up and down during the pregnancy, with patience and understanding, this is no reason to quit doing it.

For couples in high-risk pregnancies, or in cases where the woman has a history of early miscarriages, sexual intercourse may be restricted. Talk to your physician. Even in these situations, though, it may be possible for one partner to pleasure the other without having intercourse.

These sorts of sexual anxieties are common among pregnant couples. Some feel these things deeply, while some only think about them in passing. Some other common worries about intercourse during this time include the following:

- The fetus is somehow aware of its parents having sex.
- When it penetrates the vagina, the penis will puncture the amniotic sac.
- Having sex early in a normal pregnancy will stimulate a woman to go into premature labor.
- Having sex in the ninth month of a normal pregnancy will cause a woman to go into labor.
- The penis may penetrate so deeply it will touch the head of the baby.

Most of your worries, although common, are unfounded. Speak to a physician if you have concerns about sex, even if these concerns seem trivial or embarrassing. One thing you do not have to worry about, however, is your partner's getting pregnant while she is still pregnant. This is one long-held belief that is absolutely true. With no need to worry about birth control for the moment, both the man and woman often feel sexually free for the first time in a long while. This can allow them to open up and really enjoy sex.

FACT

> For most of the pregnancy, the mother and child are protected from infection as long as the man does not have a sexually transmittable disease. But in the ninth month, the amniotic sac that holds the baby could rupture at any time, exposing him to potentially harmful organisms. Some experts recommend using a condom in the final one to two months of pregnancy.

Holding and Cuddling

When making love, men tend to focus on doing the deed—sexual intercourse. Women tend to prefer foreplay—the things that lead up to doing the deed. When your partner becomes pregnant, if you are truly interested in arousing her sexually, you will need to focus even more heavily on foreplay.

For some men, this is a joy and a blessing, not a curse. They are turned on by the full-figured shape of their pregnant partner and are happy to oblige her. For other men, foreplay may be seen as more of a chore.

What Women Are Feeling

There are many reasons that pregnant women cannot jump into bed and instantly start making mad passionate love. For one thing, they cannot jump. Depending how far along they are in the pregnancy, even walking may be uncomfortable for them. For another, they are often bone-tired. All they want to do in bed is sleep.

A pregnant woman often does not feel at ease in her body. Her back hurts, her feet hurt, and her whole body is a bundle of small and not-so-small aches and pains. Later in the pregnancy she may experience some vaginal discomfort with penetration. All of this may have made her less interested in sex—and may have turned her off to it altogether.

Take It Easy

The best lovemaking approach for a pregnant woman is to simply hold her and touch her in a nonsexual way at first. Cuddle with her in bed. Rub her back and shoulders. Run your fingers along her skin and belly. Avoid touching, as long as you can, her breasts and vaginal area.

Want to give a gift to your partner? Give her a foot massage. Even if the rest of her body is uncomfortable, she will almost assuredly respond to gentle rubbing of her feet. Your technique is less important than the fact that you are willing to do it, and she will appreciate it.

Finding a Comfortable Position

Comfortable and enjoyable sexual positions will change, depending on how far along the pregnancy is. In the early stages, you can be on top of your partner. As she gets bigger and bigger, this will be less and less comfortable for you both. You may continue to be on top of her for a while if you hold yourself above her with your arms like you're doing a push-up, but eventually this will not work anymore.

The reverse—her on top, you on the bottom—may also work well. This gives her a little more control, which may help her relax. And your body weight won't be pressing against her stomach.

You will notice, as the pregnancy develops, that you will be sharing your bed with pillows that your partner is using to make herself comfortable.

These pillows come in a variety of shapes: wedges to support her growing belly, cylinders for her neck, and other types of pillows that may make your side of the bed slightly smaller. She can use these pillows to help her get into a comfortable position. If she is comfortable and enjoying herself, and you are doing the same, you know you are doing something right.

Variations to Try

Another popular position for pregnant couples is doggie-style, as it is known. The woman is on her hands and knees, supporting her abdomen with pillows. You can get behind her and enter her vaginally. But again, as the months go by and she gets bigger, she may grow less comfortable with this position.

A popular pregnancy position in the later months is spooning. This is when a couple lies on their sides in bed, the man behind the woman. Spooning is effective because her body is completely supported by the bed. She may place one of those crazy pillows she has between her knees to get more comfortable.

Touching and Oral Sex

Of course, there are ways to satisfy your partner and yourself without having intercourse. This is true for pregnant couples as well. You can simulate intercourse between her thighs or breasts, with no vaginal penetration.

ESSENTIAL

Your partner may feel physical discomfort during sex. This discomfort may be caused by a variety of reasons. She needs to listen to her body so she can let you in on how she's feeling, and you need to listen to what she says. You may need to pause or stop in the middle of things if she doesn't feel right.

Oral sex is another option. Cunnilingus—stimulating the woman's genitalia with your mouth and tongue—is safe as long as you do not blow any air into her vagina. Doing this could cause an obstruction in a blood vessel and be dangerous for both mother and child. Fellatio—her mouth on your penis—is always safe and frequently rewarding. Masturbation is yet another alternative to intercourse.

Toward a New Intimacy

Having a child can create friction. Almost immediately, your relations with your partner began to change when she became pregnant. Your sex life is one of the biggest areas of change, possibly making life between the sheets less secure and more challenging.

Amidst these challenges, opportunities exist—opportunities for greater intimacy between you and your partner. The two of you now share something you did not before: your child, another human being. This bond may lead you both to find a deeper level of commitment, physically and emotionally, in your relationship.

Your sexual activities may not be as frequent or as active as they were before your partner became pregnant. As your partner's body continues to change, these changes may dampen her sex drive and make the act of intercourse uncomfortable for her. You may also secretly worry about having sex with her at this time. But taking your time and finding comfortable positions can ease your anxieties and help make sex during pregnancy a pleasurable experience for you both.

CHAPTER 12

Making Sound Decisions

When you first learn you are going to be a father, you have nine months or so to get your act together and prepare to have a baby. In that time, you will face a number of important issues with your partner. This chapter discusses some of these issues and how to work together to make the decisions that are right for you.

Speak Up: It's Your Child, Too

Most guys have no problem making their opinion known and heard. Ask them who they think is going to win the Super Bowl or the World Series, and they'll tell you in no uncertain terms. If you happen to disagree with their point of view, they will tell you flat out how wrong you are.

When the subject turns to babies, however, these same loud-mouthed, bull-headed guys sometimes turn into pussycats. They more or less follow what their partner says and express no opinions themselves because they feel that this whole baby business is, well, a woman's thing. To some extent this is understandable. Virtually all of the action is occurring inside your partner's body, not yours, so how are you supposed to know what to do?

Some of this timidity among men may also stem from how they were raised. It may have been that their mother ran the house, made all the decisions, and was the dominant force in the family. Meanwhile their father was working at his job, wasn't around the house that much, and perhaps wasn't all that interested in what was going on anyway. Based on these role models, some fathers-to-be may figure that they, too, are supposed to step back and let their partner run the show.

One of the problems with this approach is that there are lots of decisions that need to be made when you have a baby. Your partner can indeed decide some of the minor ones with little input from you, but many of the decisions being made are huge. They are going to affect not just your partner's or your baby's life, but your life, too. You can sit on the sidelines and say nothing, or you can have a voice in these decisions. Regardless of how fathers handled it in the past, most fathers today choose to speak up.

Naming the Little One

Almost unfailingly, every parent-to-be will have an opinion on what they want to name their child. Virtually no one, male or female, stays quiet on this issue. It's too big, too important.

You intrinsically know that you are making a decision that will affect your child for the rest of his life. Wherever he goes, whatever he does, he is going to carry his name around with him. It will influence how he views himself and how others view him. Finding the right name for your child is fun, exciting, and a little humbling, too.

QUOTE

"If you are concerned about names that kids will make fun of," says Scott Lynn, father of two, "make sure you say out loud the first and last names you're thinking about before you decide. I really liked the name Amanda, but when we said the full name out loud, Amanda Lynn, it sounded like the instrument. We decided against that one."

Some Things to Consider

The name you choose for your child will in some way reflect your values as parents. Scary thought, eh? Once upon a time you may have considered yourself a free and unencumbered happy-go-lucky guy who didn't have to worry about such a boring and staid concept as "values." But times have changed, and now you are about to affix a name to another human being. There are many things to consider as you do this. Do you want the name to:

- Be a reflection of your family or ethnic heritage?
- Honor a certain family member or person?
- Be similar to your own name or a junior?
- Be relatively common or something out of the ordinary?
- Be a traditional or unusual spelling?
- Be easy for other people to pronounce and spell?
- Be a name that other children won't tease him about when he gets older?

Some parents happen to hear a name and like it and decide to use it. Others refer to the mountains of books and websites devoted to the topic. Still others may have had a name in mind since they were young, knowing that if they ever had a girl, Emily is what they'd like to name her. Some couples wait to see the baby before making a final decision on a name. Whatever the name you choose, it will always reflect your values and beliefs.

Enter the Family

One of the things that usually occurs when you have a baby is that your partner's family and your family become more involved in your lives. In some cases, "involvement" is too mild a word. A more precise word to describe what they do might be "interfere." In any case, the extended family often enters the discussion about possible names.

It is not uncommon for family members to suggest a name they like. Usually (but not always) this name is a reflection of their values and past, and it is not what you had in mind for your child. One way to handle this is to be noncommittal, saying that you and your partner are considering a bunch of names and haven't decided on anything yet. Or you may feel comfortable enough to simply say thanks, but no thanks.

FACT

The most popular name for girls in 2008 was Emma. For the eleven years before that, it was Emily. From 1970 to 1995, three girls' names were No. 1: Jessica, Ashley, and Jennifer. The most popular boys' name of the past decade was Jacob. And the most popular boys' name for the thirty-seven years before that? That was Michael.

You and Your Partner

Even without their direct involvement, family—hers and yours—can still participate in these naming discussions. For example, you may feel strongly that your son's name should be Joseph, a tribute to your Uncle Joe who was like a second father to you after your own father ran off to Tahiti with his secretary and was never heard from again. But your partner may hate that name and frankly not care all that much for Joe himself, who drinks too much and whose breath always smells like cheap Scotch.

Your partner, on the other hand, may want to choose a name that honors her parents' or grandparents' roots. Of course, she may not have said one word about her roots for all the years you two have been together, but that doesn't matter. When you have a baby, these issues suddenly come up because people identify more closely with their heritage and their past.

It is possible that you and your partner, for a variety of reasons, will disagree on your child's name. Sometimes disagreements over a name or other matters else can mask larger issues regarding your relationship. Try to find a compromise that works for both of you.

Should There Be a Junior?

A traditional male thing to do is to name your son after yourself. Some men immediately say "no" to this concept. They have never been particularly happy with their own names, and they would not think of weighing down their children with a similar burden.

Other men (and some women, too) want their child's name to be a reflection of their own. The television sports commentator and former professional athlete Deion Sanders feminized his first name and gave it to his daughter. Her name is Deiondra.

Barbecue grill-master and former heavyweight boxing champion George Foreman solved the naming issue quite simply. He has six sons, and he named them all George—George I, II, III, IV, V, and VI. It is not known what George the Elder would have done if one of his kids had been a girl.

It may be that your father named you after himself, making you a junior. The decision you and your partner must make is whether to continue with this family tradition or break it and start a new one. You may want to talk to your own father and mother about this, if you can. Sometimes the older generation does not feel as strongly about tradition as you might think, and will want you to make your own choices.

How Much Do You Tell Other People?

With just about every decision you make during pregnancy, you often have to make another decision related to it—that is, whether you should tell other people. How much do your friends and family need to know, and if you choose to tell them something, when should you do it? These are questions every couple grapples with when they have a baby.

For instance, do you tell people the due date? Letting them know the expected date of delivery helps them share the excitement of the pregnancy and plan accordingly. And yet, as the date approaches, some of these people will call the house asking if the baby has arrived, unintentionally bugging your partner at a time when she is already feeling tense enough.

Then there is the potentially big issue of the baby's name. If you and your partner have decided on her name, should you let others in on the secret? If you do, you possibly open yourself up to unexpected reactions from the people you are confiding in. They may not like the name you have chosen and bluntly tell you so. Then they may offer their own suggestions that you despise.

Or perhaps you have not settled on a name yet and you decide to confide in your best buddy with the choices you're considering. He may laugh out loud at one or two of the names you tell him—the ones you secretly like. Then what do you do? He's just doing what you asked—being honest—but in your mind he's acting like a jerk.

Many couples do reveal the due date or the name they have chosen. Others respond to questions with a vague or elusive answer—"The baby is due in early February," or "We are still discussing names." Don't let your friends or family pressure you into revealing more information than you are comfortable with. If they persist with questions you don't want to answer, simply explain that you prefer to keep that information under wraps for the time being.

Home Birth versus Hospital

Until relatively recent times, nearly all births took place at home, and this is still true in many parts of the world. In the United States and Canada, however, most couples prefer to give birth in a hospital, primarily because they feel it is safer than at home. If an emergency arises and medical intervention is required, the mother and child can receive immediate attention.

Nevertheless, some couples may consider having their child at home under the guidance of a licensed nurse-midwife. If you are interested in this option, check to see if home birth services are covered under your health care policy, and if they are, to what extent. If you have to pay out of pocket for home birth services, this could affect your decision.

ALERT

If you and your partner are considering having the baby at home, you both need to talk to her obstetrician about it. You should also talk to other parents who have had home births. As your partner's labor coach, you may feel more comfortable at a hospital with lots of medical backup close at hand. Whatever your feelings, they need to be part of the discussion.

The Gripe Against Hospitals

Some parents criticize hospitals for being insensitive to their needs. They feel that the hospital environment is cold, impersonal, and not in tune with the "natural" act of having a baby. They also feel that doctors and nurses sometimes follow a strict medical protocol regardless of the wishes of the parents, particularly those of the laboring mother. For these reasons and others, they choose to give birth at home.

Partly in response to such criticism, many hospitals and medical facilities have made a concerted effort to be more welcoming to new parents. For example, many have built labor and delivery rooms that resemble suites at the Sheraton. Before they come to the hospital, each couple prepares a "birth plan" (covered later in this chapter), which explains, in writing, how they want the birth to proceed. Physicians and nurses use this plan to guide them and—it is hoped—provide parents with a satisfactory birthing experience.

Having the Birth You Both Want

It is important to realize that you can make choices about how you want the birth to proceed, even if you choose to give birth in a hospital. You have a voice in what goes on—assuming, that is, you use it.

Your partner may have strong opinions on certain subjects. Though the birth is taking place in a hospital, she may want to have as natural a delivery as possible, without an epidural or pain medication. Then again, she may be afraid of the pain and want that medication as quickly as they will let her have it. It has become increasingly more common for pregnant women to jump-start the birth by taking drugs to induce labor rather than waiting for it to happen.

You may have strong opinions on all these subjects. You may not want to have the birth at home, if your partner is thinking along those lines. You may want her to consider pain medication and not be so dead-set against it. Or, if she's the opposite type, you may need to remind her that she will need to labor awhile before she receives an epidural—if it is given too early, it may stall her progress.

FACT

It has been stated that more than 80 percent of all mothers use some form of pain medication during childbirth. For most of these women, the medication was an epidural. About 20 percent of the mothers surveyed said they used no pain medication.

As your partner's birth coach, one of your jobs is to talk to her about all these things. Think these issues through—big and small—and try to work them out together. Whatever the two of you decide and are comfortable with, that is the way to do it.

Ultimately, however, you and your partner must make these decisions. There is no way to avoid them because the baby is coming, ready or not. And it is far better to be ready than to wait until the last minute.

Developing a Birth Plan

Despite amazing advances in technology and medical science, having a baby remains a mysterious act. So much about it is not known. No one knows, for example, what triggers the onset of labor. The full moon? The changing of the tides? Theories and superstitions abound.

Another truth about childbirth is that it is impossible to control. Things happen in the process of labor and delivery that no one can predict. Each child's birth follows a pattern similar to every other child's birth, and yet it is different too. There are lots and lots of variables.

One way that you and your partner can get a handle on these two elements—what is unknown and what cannot be controlled—is to form a birth plan. A birth plan is a one- or two-page written statement that you create with the help of your partner's doctor and present to the hospital or birthing center when you arrive to deliver the baby. Your partner will probably write the first draft of the plan, and you will absolutely want to review it and discuss with her any changes you want to make. A birth plan tells your goals and desires, briefly explaining such basics as:

- Who the birth coach is
- Who else will be in the room besides the coach
- Whether your partner wants to be connected to an intravenous drip or have electronic fetal monitoring
- Techniques such as walking around, sitting up, and showering to be used to keep labor from stalling
- Views on the use and types of pain medication
- "Red flags" the hospital should know about, such as possible complications with the pregnancy
- What the atmosphere of the room should be: music, lights dimmed, aromatherapy, etc.
- The father cutting the umbilical cord
- The mother taking the baby to her breast and holding her before the cord is cut or other procedures take place
- "Rooming in:" the baby staying with the mother at all times or going to a nursery outside her room

A birth plan is not an absolute. Your wishes must conform to hospital procedures. For example, some hospitals do not allow CD players to be plugged into their electrical wall outlets; therefore, if you want music, you must plan ahead to bring a battery-operated CD player or iPod. Check with the hospital ahead of time on its policies.

As detailed and complete as your birth plan may be, you should always leave room for the unexpected. The one thing you can count on in childbirth is that things will not proceed as you expect. Be prepared to make changes and to act on unanticipated developments.

Circumcision

Circumcision is the surgical removal of the fold of skin (the foreskin) that covers the penis. About one-third to one-half of the foreskin is cut off, often in the hospital following birth. In some religions, such as Judaism, the procedure is also performed as part of a ritual by an approved practitioner within a week or so after birth. Nevertheless, most couples make the circumcision decision well in advance of their son's arrival.

FACT

Approximately 55 to 60 percent of all boys born today in the United States are circumcised; the remaining 40 percent are left intact. Outside the United States, circumcision is commonly practiced in Israel and Islamic nations. In Europe, Africa, Asia, and Latin America, circumcision is rarely performed.

Circumcision is easily one of the most volatile issues concerning baby boys. Both sides—pro and con—get extremely worked up about it, marshalling an array of heated arguments to back up their points of view. For obvious reasons, this issue hits very close to home for men.

What Doctors Say about It

Not long ago, circumcisions were routinely performed in the United States. Virtually an entire generation of baby boomer boys were circumcised. The thinking at the time was that those children would have fewer medical problems if the foreskin was removed.

This thinking has since undergone an upheaval. The American Academy of Pediatrics has ruled that circumcision is "not medically necessary." In other words, the old justification for the procedure—that it will prevent medical problems—no longer holds.

This has not stopped the battle, however. Both sides adamantly point to studies that support their views. Those in favor say circumcision can significantly reduce the risk of urinary tract infections and the transmission of some sexual diseases. They compare circumcision to immunization in its prevention of certain diseases and infections.

The other side rejects this argument, saying that the foreskin is a piece of the man's body and that cutting it off is "unnecessary surgery." They argue that problems can be prevented by adequate cleaning. They also cite studies demonstrating that circumcised males experiment more with alternative sexual practices than intact ones, and that these practices can lead to disease. With so many questions and controversy surrounding the practice, they conclude, the prudent and safe thing is not to do it.

Adding to the emotional nature of this argument is the cultural and religious side of it. Both Jews and Muslims practice circumcision as an integral part of their faiths.

Like Father, Like Son

Fathers-to-be are encouraged to read about circumcision and find out the facts. Even though you may be circumcised yourself, you may not have thought that much about it. You can weigh the evidence and decide for yourself whether or not to snip.

Many men, though, are going to ask themselves a simple question: do I want my son to look like me? How you answer this question may determine what you decide to do. If you are circumcised, and you want your son to look like you, you will ask to have the procedure done.

It does not matter that you and your son will almost assuredly *not* be standing around comparing your penises. Many men still want their son to look like them. If your penis is intact, however, chances are you will want to keep your son's the same way.

QUESTION

What if my partner disagrees with me about circumcision?
You're going to have to listen to her point of view. You may feel that being a man entitles you to decide this issue, but it doesn't always work that way. She may have strong feelings, too.

Birth Control

Another big issue that needs to be discussed is birth control. Are you going to have another child after this one? Although it may seem premature to talk about this issue, you may resume sexual relations with your partner as early as six weeks after the baby is born. What are you going to do then?

Some people believe that if a woman is breastfeeding, she cannot become pregnant. Some also believe that if a woman has not resumed menstruating after having a baby, she cannot get pregnant. Neither is true. You need to take precautions when you start having sex; otherwise, you may find yourself in this fix again sooner than you anticipate.

Many couples decide to have more than one child. Even those who end up only having one often do not immediately know what they want to do. Having a baby can be overwhelming at first, and it takes time to figure out whether you want your child to have a brother or sister.

ESSENTIAL

When talking with your partner about birth control or anything else, remember that not every discussion needs to lead to a plan of action or an immediate solution. Just sitting down together and airing your thoughts may be all that needs to be done at the moment.

Your partner especially will need to rest and recover after the baby comes. You will both need to make adjustments to this major new development in your lives. All of that takes time, and there is no need to rush into having another child.

This all leads back to the subject of birth control. It may be that this was an unplanned pregnancy—that your partner was on the pill or using a diaphragm when it happened. Or perhaps you happened to forget to put on the condom that night. In any case, it may be wise to review your birth control techniques and think about a different approach.

CHAPTER 13

Preparing Your Home and Car

It makes sense to be ready for the big day. Doing a few practical things around the house or apartment will help your partner relax, and it may reassure you as well. Here are some ways to prepare your home and car before the baby arrives and everything goes nuts.

The Nesting Instinct

While living with their pregnant partners, many fathers-to-be have observed what can only be described as "the nesting instinct." Often women focus intently on their surroundings and feel a strong need to fix up their home or apartment to get it ready for the baby. Sometimes this feeling can make Mom frustrated with her current abode. If she lives in an apartment, she may want to look into buying a house. If she already lives in a house, she may want to get into a bigger one.

These nesting urges on the part of your partner, while common among pregnant women, may feel like another degree of pressure squeezing in on you. If she suddenly starts talking about moving to a bigger place, this represents an obvious financial challenge. With her about to leave her job for an indefinite time due to the pregnancy, the burden of paying an increased rent or mortgage will likely fall largely on your shoulders, at least in the beginning. You may not be ready for a change of this magnitude, and you need to tell her that.

Your partner's nesting feelings may crop up in other ways as well. She probably does not want to go out very much at night or even on the weekends. This is partly because she is tired and perhaps uncomfortable in her body, but it's also because she wants to stay home, where she feels more comfortable. This tendency will only get stronger the closer she gets to her due date.

Men don't talk about it much, but many of them have nesting feelings too. The instinct is not nearly as strong as their partner's, perhaps, but many fathers-to-be also feel a pull toward home during the final months of pregnancy. To some degree, this is due to the needs of the mother, who wants the father-to-be close by and able to respond if something happens. This is a time when many men cancel or postpone work-related trips that may take them far from home.

These nesting feelings serve a valuable purpose. They motivate both you and your partner to get your home in order. You do not have to move into a mansion or build a new wing on the house because you are having a baby. But a few simple things need to be taken care of and once they are, you and your partner will feel more at ease.

Fixing Up the Nursery

From the man's point of view, one nice thing about fixing up the nursery is that you actually get to do something. For the father-to-be, so much of the pregnancy consists of waiting . . . and waiting . . . and waiting. Not much happens directly to you, and there is not a whole heckuva lot to do. The nursery gives you a chance to break out a can of paint and get your hands dirty.

QUESTION

What if my partner wants to do something I don't like?
Let her know, but give her an alternative. If you know you're having a boy, and she wants to paint the nursery pink, suggest that a more gender-neutral color, such as yellow or green, may be more appropriate. She will be more open to you if she doesn't feel criticized.

Many parents-to-be, of course, do not have a separate room for a nursery. They make do by using a portion of their own bedroom or another room. It may not be ideal, but it works just fine and the baby doesn't care one whit. He and all the gear related to him are basically going to take over your whole place anyway.

Reporting for Duty

It may be that you are an interior decorator at heart and have elaborate ideas on the colors and look of your baby's nursery. It is more likely, however, that you have not given this subject one thought in your entire life. Almost certainly, your partner will take the lead in this area, and you will follow. She will be the head designer and make the big decisions. You will be the laborer. So it goes.

Expect there to be several changes to her design scheme before she settles on a final look. She may want to sample different paint colors to see which ones she likes. She may want to call in outside consultants—her mother and friends—to help her with her decision-making process. She will likely ask you what you think.

For many women, putting together their child's nursery is a little like planning a wedding. They have certain ideas and expectations on how they want things to be, and these feelings are quite strong and will often manifest in their emotions.

Safety First

While you may be willing to go along with your partner's design scheme for the nursery, the one area that you cannot be silent about is safety. The safety of your child's surroundings is your number-one consideration. It takes precedence over everything else.

ESSENTIAL

Painting and fixing up the nursery is a good middle-trimester project, say around the sixth or seventh month. Paint the nursery well in advance of the baby's arrival—you want the room to air out completely before he has to sleep in it. You do not want him breathing harmful paint fumes.

Look around at the placement of the crib and the arrangement of furniture in the room. Do you see any potential hazards? If you live in an earthquake-prone area, do not place a heavy clothes dresser where it could fall over and hit the crib. Bolt it solidly to the wall. Also, do not place a bookshelf with lots of knickknacks above the crib for the same reason.

Building a Crib

When the baby first comes home, she will almost certainly not sleep in a crib. She is so tiny, and the crib is so big. For the first few months she will sleep in a bassinet or perhaps your own bed or a co-sleeper.

Sooner or later, though, your child will move into her crib. This is where she will spend much of her day asleep. She will be alone during this time, not watched by either her mother or you. For these reasons, her crib needs to be absolutely safe.

Used Cribs

As many as three out of four newborns in the United States sleep in used cribs. You may receive a loaner from other parents who no longer need theirs. You may have picked one up at a yard or garage sale. Grandma may have also given you a sentimental hand-me-down. She may have kept the crib you slept in when you were a baby for decades, waiting for the chance to give it to you so you could use it for your child.

There is absolutely nothing wrong with a used crib, as long as it is safe. A used crib may have been sitting in a garage for years, gathering dust. Parts may need to be replaced, and it may need a new paint job. Check it over thoroughly. You may need to refurbish part or all of it before you let your baby sleep in it.

Safety Checklist

Most crib injuries occur when the child is older and can move around. The baby could jump up and down and catch a piece of clothing on a corner post extension, causing strangulation. Or she could jump with enough force to make the entire crib collapse on top of her. Both of these are frightening scenarios, to be sure, but they can and do occur.

Your child will not be able to jump or bounce or move around in her crib for some months. You will put her down on her back, and that is how she will be when you return to pick her up after her nap. Even so, your crib needs to be safe from day one. Here are some guidelines to follow:

- Shake the crib after you assemble it. Make sure it is solid and not wobbly.
- Inspect corner extensions. Corner posts need to be the same height as end panels so clothing cannot catch on them.
- Remove corner post extensions if they stick out. Saw them off and sand them down.
- Inspect the slats, which must be less than $2\frac{3}{8}$ inches apart. A child will stick her feet down in the slats and may wedge her head in the spaces.
- Tighten down the screws, nuts, and hardware. They should be solidly in place and secure.

- Check for any sharp edges or points or any rough surfaces. Sand them down smooth.
- Be sure the mattress fits snugly. Babies can slip into the gaps between the mattress and crib and suffocate.
- Follow the instructions if putting together a new crib. A badly assembled crib may lead to problems.
- Inspect the crib periodically. Screws can become loose, especially when the baby gets older and more active.

If you have any doubts about your crib, junk it and get a new one. If that's not possible, hire someone to take a look at it and fix what needs to be fixed. Your baby needs a safe crib, and knowing you have provided this for her will give you peace of mind.

FACT

Thousands of children are hurt in unsafe cribs every year. Many of these injuries are so severe that the infants need medical treatment. More seriously, hundreds of children have died in the past decade from injuries sustained in their crib. The causes of many of these injuries and deaths are considered preventable. To check recalls visit *www.cpsc.gov.*

The Family Bed

An increasing number of couples do not use a bassinet or crib. Instead, they let their newborn sleep in bed with them. This is called "the family bed"—Mom, Dad, and baby, all sleeping together.

How does this work out? Well, it depends on the family. Some fathers love sleeping with their infant children. They may be gone at work and not see their family all day long. Being able to share a bed with them at night makes them feel connected to them.

Family bed advocates believe that it promotes family togetherness as well as a greater sense of well-being for the child. The child is not alone in a crib or bassinet; he is cuddled up with his mother and father, sharing their bodily warmth. This, say the family bed people, comforts him and makes him feel more secure. Some parents like sleeping with their child because it is truly something you can only do when he is little. When he grows older and bigger, he will likely have to move into a crib.

Many men, however, are not too keen on the family bed concept. They are often the ones who have to get up early in the morning to go to work. They need a good night's sleep—as good as they can get, anyhow—and they do not want to hear every peep and cry and gurgle their newborn makes. Family beds frequently turn into fatherless beds because the man leaves to sack out on the living room couch.

Men worry about possibly rolling over on top of their child. Even if it doesn't happen, the thought of it causes them to lose sleep. Some men also see their time in bed with their partners as precious. Even if they do not make love, they can talk and be intimate with her. The baby's presence in bed can interfere with this.

ALERT

Never let your newborn sleep on a waterbed. The mattress should be firm, with no folds or spaces in the bedding that might affect her breathing. Remember that alcohol can deaden your senses when you are asleep. You should not sleep in the same bed with an infant after you've been drinking.

If either you or your partner care to sleep with the baby, you may want to give it a try to see how it works. One advantage is that when the baby cries in the middle of the night and needs to be fed, neither of you has to stand up to get him. Your partner slips him her breast, and he quiets down. A device called a "co-sleeper" could be a good compromise. It sits next to your partner's side of the bed. When the baby is done nursing, she slides him onto the co-sleeper, allowing him to be close to the two of you but in a separate space.

Babyproofing Your Home

Fortunately, this is one thing you do not need to worry about during pregnancy. Your baby is tucked safely inside his mother's body and cannot yet crawl around and pull books off the bookshelf or jimmy with the knobs on your CD player. This is something you have to look forward to.

You can easily wait until your baby is two to four months old before childproofing your home. Basically, you want to make sure that where you live is a safe environment for your child to move around in and explore. Here are a few childproofing basics:

- Move objects on shelves out of child's reach.
- Attach childproof latches to drawers you do not want your child to get into.
- Install safety gates at top and bottom of stairs.
- Attach corner cushions to sharp-edged tables, furniture, and brick fireplaces.
- Put on stove knob covers and other oven safety devices. Use the back burners when cooking on the stove.
- Install a toilet guard so the child cannot lift the lid.
- Insert plugs in all electrical outlets.
- Put breakable dishes out of reach or lock them up.
- Make sure all medicine, cleaning products, garden fertilizer, and pesticides are locked up and out of reach.

Childproof products are available at hardware stores, grocery stores, specialty children's stores, and many other places. Once your child begins to move around, you will be amazed at how creative she will be at getting into potentially hazardous situations. Take your eyes off her for one second, and suddenly she's into something she shouldn't be. That is why childproofing is necessary.

QUOTE

When the time comes for babyproofing, Lance Sommerfeld, father of one and the organizer of a fathers' group, has a good tip: "One helpful piece of advice that was given to me is 'to crawl around on all fours like your child to see what they see' so you can find trouble areas." It is not bad advice for talking with your children, too. Sit down with them on the floor or wherever so you can be on their level, rather than always standing above them dictating to them.

In the Event of an Emergency

Accidents are the leading cause of injury and death among children, far exceeding disease and illness. The causes include electrical shock, drowning, swallowing foreign objects or poisonous substances, fire, burns, and car crashes. More children are injured and die in car accidents than any other cause. Close calls and accidents of any kind will require fast thinking and action on your part.

Infant CPR

Most parents will never have to use CPR techniques on their children, but babies are putting things in their mouth all the time—things they find on the carpet, things they find in the yard—and they can easily choke. Babies can accidentally fall into a pool or shallow water and be unable to get out. Babies can also experience breathing difficulties at times.

Pregnancy is a good time to take an infant CPR class because you're motivated to learn as much as you can. Learning the ABCs—airway, breathing, circulation—of emergency life-resuscitation techniques is a life skill that will have benefits for a long time to come.

Certainly your day care person, if you use one, needs to know how to perform CPR on an infant. It should be one of the questions you ask before you leave your child with her. She should take CPR refresher courses every year to keep up to date.

ESSENTIAL

Infant CPR classes are widely available through local chapters of the American Red Cross and American Heart Association, hospitals and medical facilities, colleges, and day care associations. Classes are frequently held in the evenings and on Saturdays in order to make it easier for working parents to attend.

Preventing Burns

One safety measure you can take now (or soon after the baby comes) is to turn down the thermostat on your water heater. Most water heaters are normally set at around 155°F. By turning yours down to about 120 to 130 degrees, you can help prevent scalding your baby in bath water that's too hot—a common form of injury to babies.

Many burns to young children are caused not by fire but by scalding. Be careful about where you set your morning cup of coffee—a baby could knock it over and burn himself. In addition to the bath, the kitchen is a place where burn accidents frequently occur. Hot water can boil over and spill, and grease can splatter. Always be aware of where your child is.

Be wary of microwave ovens. Heating baby formula or baby food in a microwave is a bad idea. The outside of the jar can feel cool to the touch while the contents inside are boiling.

Fire Prevention

Fire prevention is another precaution you can take right now. Firefighters recommend that you test your smoke alarms every month and that you change the batteries once a year. (A good reminder might be to change them when you change the clocks for daylight-saving time every year.) You and your partner may have already discussed an escape route in the event of a fire in your home. If not, take a minute and talk it over.

Simple carelessness can cause a fire. Be sure you don't put a space heater too close to the drapes or wall. Many fires start in the kitchen, so be sure you have a fire extinguisher in the kitchen, as well as one kept perhaps in an upstairs bedroom.

Disaster Planning

This chapter includes basic safety measures that you may have already thought about and put into place in your home or apartment, but some of these procedures may need to be reviewed with the coming arrival of baby. This is a good time to do it, too, while you're still getting a full night's sleep and thinking clearly and your life and house haven't yet been turned topsy-turvy.

Disaster planning is one more area worth reviewing. If an earthquake, fire, or major winter storm struck without warning, would your family be ready for it? Basic services such as water, gas, phone, and electricity may be cut off in a crisis, and it may take hours or days to restore them. It makes sense to be prepared.

A well-stocked emergency cache includes drinking water, canned food and other imperishable food items (with a can opener), a battery-powered radio with extra batteries, a flashlight, candles and matches, clothing, blankets, sleeping bags, a Swiss Army knife, and a first-aid kit. Some cash in case you need spending money, a credit card, an extra set of car keys, and spare eyeglasses are useful items as well. Remember to pack for the baby, who will need diapers, a couple of toys, clothing, and blankets to stay warm.

Staying in Touch: The Beauty of Cell Phones

Cell phones were invented for pregnant couples to stay in touch with each other. Well, okay, that may be stretching it a little, but they are extremely useful during this time. Almost everyone has a cell these days, but if you're one of the last hold-outs, you may wish to rethink your position and get mobile service.

Not long ago, birth coaches were advised to bring lots of dimes and quarters with them when they came to the hospital for labor and delivery. After the birth, they made their calls from the pay phone in the hallway to let people know that the baby had arrived. Now, loading down your pockets with change is no longer necessary, and pay phones are steadily becoming obsolete.

You can obviously take pictures with the phone's built-in camera too. But the biggest advantage to cell phones is that they let you keep in touch with your partner as you get closer and closer to the big day. Then, when you get that panicky call from her telling you that she has indeed gone into labor and needs you to come home right away, you can respond instantaneously.

Car Seats

A car seat for baby is mandatory. You need a car seat to take your child home from the hospital. The hospital staff is required to check for one or at least ask you about it before releasing the baby into your care and letting you drive home with her.

It is wise to install your car seat a few days or a week before the due date. You never know what can happen, and the car seat is one less thing you have to think about if your partner goes into labor and you need to go to the hospital unexpectedly.

Child safety seats are credited with saving thousands of lives over the years, and law enforcement officials believe that even more lives could be saved if more parents learned to install these seats correctly. Studies have shown that nine out of ten car seats are improperly installed, exposing babies and infants to unnecessary risk.

Car Seat Basics

Your baby's weight and size determines the type of safety seat to use. The American Academy of Pediatrics recommends keeping your child in a rear-facing seat until he or she reaches 30 pounds. The car seat should be placed in the back seat, and the baby gets buckled into that.

ALERT

Passenger-side air bags in automobiles can be extremely dangerous if a child is placed in a car seat in the front seat. When the bag inflates, it can hit the back of the car seat, push it forward, and injure the child. Always buckle your child in her car seat in the back seat.

In some cases, a safety seat might not be compatible with your vehicle. Perhaps it's too large for your back seat, or a piece of the base may stick out over the seat. Whether you're getting a new or used car seat, test it and make sure it works properly before you buy it.

Sometimes the car seat will not work with the existing seat belt. You may need to buy a supplemental belt or a locking clip. Never jury-rig a car seat; if it doesn't work right, get one that does.

Find Out How to Install

Child safety seats would seem to be easy to install, but often they are not. Sometimes it is difficult to figure out how to work the car seat's straps and buckles. The child must be strapped into the car seat, and that must be held in place by the seat belt. It can be confusing.

Your local police and fire stations may be able to help you install your car seat. Or, if you've got it in, they can check to see that you've done it right.

Childbirth preparation classes sometimes offer this service. If yours doesn't, the teachers can still tell you where to get help.

Sometimes hospitals hold seminars for pregnant couples and invite police officers to check over the installation of car seats. This is usually a popular attraction for fathers-to-be. It is frequently their job to put in the car seat, and they want to make sure they do it right.

You have learned in this chapter about fixing up the nursery, building a crib, and childproofing your home. You have reviewed basic safety and emergency precautions. You have figured out what gear you need to have, and you've installed a car seat. These practical steps have given you some peace of mind and helped prepare you for the job ahead.

CHAPTER 14

Birth Coach

A father has many important jobs in a family. He is a provider, guardian, teacher, advisor, role model, disciplinarian, and nurturer. Nowadays, fathers-to-be have an added responsibility: birth coach. This chapter explains what you need to know to help your partner bring your child into the world.

What a Birth Coach Does

Millions of fathers have served as labor coaches, and these men would testify that it is one of the greatest experiences they have ever had. To see your child draw his first breath of air and to assist in his delivery—there is nothing quite like it in the world. It is demanding, nerve-wracking, exhausting, frustrating, emotionally draining—and one of the greatest natural highs a man can have. If you miss your child's birth, these men will tell you, you are truly missing out on one of life's most rewarding and enriching experiences.

Many fathers have qualms before the birth. Having only heard about it and never done it before, they may have privately wondered if they were up to the task. Once they went through it, though, they realized that they had basically been worried about nothing. They handled it just fine.

Coach as Cheerleader

The title of "labor coach" is actually a misnomer. You're more of a cheerleader than a coach. If you want to express this in sporting terms, your partner is the main player on the field. She has the ball (your child). The real coaches—the people who are going to make the ultimate decisions about what happens to your partner—are the members of the medical staff, including the doctors, nurses, nurse-midwife, and anesthesiologist. Their job is to deliver your partner and the ball safely across the goal line.

So what do you do in the meantime? You cheer your partner on. Not with rah-rah, sis-boom-bah yells, but by offering encouragement in her ear and telling her you love her.

Your Partner's Chief Advocate

Being a cheerleader is not your only job, however. Far from it. You have other, equally important jobs. One of them is serving as your partner's chief advocate, her voice amidst all the furious activity that is occurring around her.

"What's that?" you may say. "My partner has never had any trouble speaking up for herself in the past. Why does she need me to speak for her in the most important moments of her life?"

The simple answer is that she may not be able to. She may be in so much pain she cannot think straight. She may be angry or in tears or feel as if things are out of control. The nurses may have given her drugs to combat the pain, and those drugs may have made her light-headed. Various scenarios can arise in which the medical team needs to consult with you.

ESSENTIAL

You must strike a balance when dealing with the medical staff. You are not a trained physician. You have never been through this before; they have. Even so, you do have a voice and some power in this situation. Ultimately, though, the attending physicians and nurses will make the final decisions.

You and your partner have talked about how you want the delivery to proceed. You know what her wishes are. You have prepared a birth plan together. You may have her sister or a paid professional labor assistant in the room with you. All of this will help guide you as you deal with the doctors and nurses.

You can disagree with the medical staff if you do not like what is going on. The labor may have stalled, and the staff may suggest giving your partner a drug you've never heard of. They may warn that if things don't pick up, she is headed for a Cesarean section. If this isn't what you wanted, you will have to stick to your guns and tell them that you are going to keep working with your partner and doing the activities that you learned in childbirth classes to stimulate the labor and get it moving again.

Your Baby's Chief Advocate

As birth coach, you act as your partner's emotional support and her chief advocate. Not to be forgotten is your role on behalf of your unborn child. Sometimes you are his chief advocate, too.

For example, your partner may have requested an epidural in her birth plan, but her labor moved so fast that an epidural is no longer option. Despite this, she is still in extreme pain and may holler, or even beg, for an epidural.

The nurses may advise you, however, that providing pain relieving drugs for your partner at this point may slow the labor down and affect the baby's progress down the birth canal. In this case, you must do the right thing for your child, even if it contradicts the wishes of your partner. Tell her what is going on and why. Be sure she knows that the pain she is feeling is productive pain and that she is getting results. Then work with her and support her and help her to get that baby out.

You will likely be called upon to make decisions in the labor and delivery room. That is the nature of your job as labor coach. It is not a passive role, and you may be exhausted and a little light-headed and not exactly sure what the right thing to do is. Still, with the assistance of the medical team, you need to make a judgment and go with it.

Childbirth Preparation Classes

As the name implies, childbirth preparation classes are designed to get you and your partner ready for labor and delivery. They are also referred to as childbirth "education" classes—another tip-off to what they are about. Neither of you has been down this road before, and these classes may help reduce fear and worry and give you a sense of what you can expect.

Your hospital or birth center will likely offer these classes, usually for a minimal fee. Childbirth preparation classes are also sometimes taught privately by registered nurses and other instructors. You'll typically attend these classes in the seventh or eighth month of the pregnancy. Classes are usually held once a week for six to ten weeks, but some programs condense the sessions into one or two days on the weekend.

FACT

According to one study, 60 percent of all fathers-to-be who participated in childbirth education classes still chose to take a passive role during labor and delivery. Other studies, however, report much higher rates of involvement among men after taking these classes. Fathers-to-be generally perceive that their actions are very helpful to their partner during labor.

One purpose of these classes is to provide information and teach you about the process of childbirth. Some men may assume that their partners know everything there is to know about their bodies and what happens when they have a baby. This is hardly the case. Your partner may be as clueless about all of this as you are, giving you both the chance to learn together.

Indeed, this is another purpose of these classes: to foster a connection between you and your partner. You are going to have to learn how to work as a team. Another way to put it is that the two of you got into this together, and now you are going to have to get through it together, too.

Supporting Mom Physically

Another major reason for attending childbirth preparation classes is to learn specific techniques to help your partner endure the pain of labor and delivery as well as she possibly can. If you want an inkling of what it is like to have a baby, go out into the garage and stick your thumb in a vise. Then tighten the vise, and let off, and then tighten it again, and then let off, each time tightening it harder than the last. Keep doing this for, oh, the next twenty-four to thirty-six hours straight, and you will still not be close to feeling the pain of a laboring woman. You know why? Because it is not just her thumb that is absorbing this ever tightening, vise-like pain, it's her whole body.

To help her get through this ordeal, your partner is going to learn some breathing and other techniques to relax and endure the pain. Your job will be to assist her. You can help her in a variety of ways, including these:

- Walking with her, keeping her moving.
- Encouraging her to sit up, not labor lying down.
- Letting her lean on you while standing, her arms around your neck to take some of the pressure off her legs.
- Applying counter-pressure, with your hand against her lower back during a contraction.
- Helping her in and out of the tub if she wants to take a bath.
- Letting her lean on you in the shower as the hot water hits her lower back.

- Getting her glasses of water, because she will be expending a lot of energy and needs to keep her fluids up.
- Applying a cold washcloth to her forehead.

These techniques will probably work best during early labor. Later, when the labor progresses and the pain becomes more intense, it is going to be more difficult to find ways to assist her. Her focus is intensely inward, and there are many new sensations occurring inside her body. You may find that many of the techniques you learned in childbirth preparation class are useless and provide no comfort to her, but you won't know that until you're in the middle of things.

ESSENTIAL

Listen to your partner. She will tell you what she needs. Light massage may help her initially, or it may not. Or it may help in the beginning, but as the labor goes on, she may tell you that your touch irritates and distracts her. Don't take anything personally, just try to respond in the moment and do the best you can.

Providing Emotional Support

As the labor goes on (and on and on) and the pain keeps riding the up escalator, the emotional support you give your partner may be the most important thing you can do for her. First labors are almost never as quick as second labors. They can last for twelve to sixteen to twenty-four to thirty-six hours. Obviously, the longer it drags on, the more exhausted and discouraged your partner will be.

In the face of all this, your job is to tell her what a great job she is doing, how much you love her, how hard she is working, how proud you are of her, and how much progress she is making. Your goal is to buck up her spirits and keep her going. Make sure she knows she is not alone and that you are with her all the way.

The Lay of the (Hospital) Land

A standard part of childbirth education classes is the hospital tour. Led by the instructor, you and your partner and the rest of your classmates get a walkthrough of the maternity wing. Although it may feel a little like being shepherded around by your third-grade teacher on a primary school field trip, it's worthwhile to go. The tour will give you a feel for the physical layout of where your child will be born.

As the instructor leads you around, she will fill you in on hospital dos and don'ts. One issue you need to be aware of is where to park the car while you're checking your partner into her room. If it's a small hospital or medical facility, you may be able to simply park in the parking lot and walk her in. In larger hospitals, though, the only parking available is sometimes in a giant parking structure some distance away from the maternity wing. In this case, you may have to park temporarily in emergency room parking, then check in your partner and get her situated before going back out to park your car for the night.

Wheelchair for Pregnant Moms

Every hospital has its own way of doing things, but it is generally recommended that the laboring mother ride in a wheelchair once she arrives. Some laboring women resist. They say they do not need it, and they can walk just fine. Many do indeed walk all the way to the admitting room, steadying themselves on a railing along the wall.

ALERT

Sometimes you may need to insist that your partner do something that you feel she should. Other times you will need to back off and help her do it the way she wants to. You will both be stressed in these moments. Getting defensive or sulking because you did not get your way will not help the situation.

Depending on how far along her labor is, your partner will be struggling as she walks, stopping frequently whenever the pain of a contraction comes on. You might suggest to her that she is going to be working awfully hard over the next hours, and there is no reason why she cannot take it easy and accept a ride in a wheelchair. If she still says no, just help her as best as you can.

The Admitting Room

After parking your car and winding your way through to the hospital, at some point you will reach the admitting room. You have already called ahead to the hospital to let them know you're coming, so they have already pulled your partner's medical chart. You are carrying copies of your birth plan, so you give one to the nurse to attach to the chart. The admitting room is where the hospital will decide whether to book you a room for the night.

QUOTE

During labor, says Greg Bishop, a father of four and a professional birth advisor for fathers, "moms often feel like they're losing control over their bodies. When pain and emotions like these are taking center stage, expecting her to keep track of whether or not the birth plan is being followed, or if the private room she requested is available, is just too much. It is in this area where Dads can step up and make her feel supported, by handling details and speaking up for her."

The Labor and Delivery Room

Once you're admitted, you and your partner will be assigned to a labor and delivery room. Its main feature is a hospital bed (or "birthing bed"), where your partner will be attached to a machine that monitors her contractions, the baby's heart rate, and other vital signs. Your partner will also be hooked into an IV pole to make sure she gets the fluids she needs. Intravenous infusion is also used to administer pain medicine.

There will likely be a large chair and a TV in the room, although these are not to be used for kicking back and watching the game. Sometimes you will need to get your partner up and walk her around with that cumbersome IV pole, or escort her to the bathroom where she can stand in the shower, lean against the wall, and let the hot water hit her back to relieve some of the pain.

More Stops on the Tour

Another stop on the hospital tour is the lunch or beverage room. Your partner may never see this room while she is in labor, but you will likely visit it several times. You will use this room to get ice chips for your partner (some women like to suck on them to quench their thirst) and ice-cold water from a refrigerated dispenser. There is likely a hot-water pot for coffee or tea and a refrigerator where labor coaches can store their food.

Sometimes on the tour they take you past the door of the neonatal intensive care unit. Premature babies and babies who have problems at birth are brought to this room, where they are cared for by highly trained, dedicated, and motivated physician-specialists and nurses. You will not be allowed to go into this room, and you may not even want to think about any circumstances in which your child would have to go there. At the very least, it is comforting to know that the neonatal ICU is close by if anything does happen.

The Nursery

The nursery is the show-stopping highlight of every hospital tour. It is where the newborns are kept if they are not in the room with Mom. Everybody on the tour stands outside the window, grinning like idiots. Even at this late date in the pregnancy, it is still hard to fathom that you and your partner are soon going to have one of those soon.

What to Bring to the Hospital

Television sitcoms and movies often rely on some standard goofy jokes when they tell stories involving women in labor and the well-meaning but bumbling men in their life. One of these jokes has to do with a woman who is having big contractions and needs to go to the hospital—pronto! In his haste and confusion, the father jumps into the car and drives off without her. Only after he is on the road does he realize his mistake.

One reason why this scenario never occurs in real life is that it is impossible to forget about your laboring partner, mostly because she will not let you drive off without her. Here are some other items that you dare not forget when you take your partner to the hospital to have a baby:

- A car seat for your child
- Multiple copies of your birth plan
- Your partner's overnight bag stocked with her toiletries, nightgown, set of comfortable clothes, nursing bra, and other items she needs
- Juice, broth, and light snacks for her
- Food for you—sandwiches, fruit, energy bars, tea, coffee
- Birthing ball, massage tools, hot or cold packs, or any other birthing aids that you need to assist her in labor
- CD player and CDs, aromatherapy materials to make the room the way she wants it (assuming the hospital permits this)
- Cell phone, charged and ready for action with key phone numbers listed in the memory
- Camcorder and still camera (or camera phone)

You need to dress comfortably—you may be in those clothes for a long time. Wear running shoes or shoes that give you plenty of support because you will be on your feet a lot. Giving birth is a kind of marathon, so you need to prepare yourself for the long haul and bring whatever you need to help you and your partner make it to the finish line.

Having a Family Member Assist You

Many fathers who have served as labor coaches heartily recommend bringing in another person to assist during labor and delivery. It is another pair of hands that can help out during this turbulent time. If the labor goes on for many hours, you can cover for each other when one of you needs a break. This person can also provide valuable counsel. If a decision needs to be made, it is often useful to hear the opinion of someone you know and who knows you well, too.

Some fathers who served as their partner's only labor coach for their first child choose to bring in another person for the birth of their second child. While continuing as their partner's coach, they know from experience that labor can be an overwhelming experience and that another person in the room can be extremely useful. In short, it makes their job easier.

ALERT

Make sure your co-coach is a team player who will work together with you. Avoid high-maintenance personalities who may agitate or upset you or your partner.

An obvious candidate for your birth team is someone from your partner's family—her sister or perhaps her mother. Your partner may have a friend whom she feels close to and request her presence. First talk to this person to see if she is interested. While she probably does not need to attend classes she may need to do some homework on the subject if she has never participated in childbirth before. The three of you will need to get together at least once before the birth to plot strategy and be clear about your roles.

Hiring a Professional Labor Assistant

Another option worth considering is hiring a doula, or professional labor assistant. The word "doula" derives from the Greek term meaning "in service." This is a good explanation of what a doula does. She is in service to your partner and you, helping you in a variety of nonmedical ways.

A doula is not a medical person. She is not trained in medicine, nor can she advise you on medical matters. She is not a hospital employee, but rather is hired by you to provide physical and emotional support during the birthing experience. The cost usually ranges from $300 to $500, with most doulas charging somewhere in the middle of the range.

What a Doula Does

Doulas cite evidence that shows labor tends to be shorter, far fewer drugs are used, forceps delivery occurs much less, and the Cesarean rate is cut virtually in half when they are present at births. They say that their presence can make the labor less arduous and provide a better birthing experience for women. Doulas are almost all women, and they are frequently mothers who decided to become birth assistants after going through childbirth themselves. Most have assisted at dozens of births.

What does a doula do? She helps the mother focus on her breathing and concentration. She gets her to sit up in bed and change positions in order to keep the labor progressing. She will bring a bag of birthing aids to assist the mother. One of these may be a birthing ball, a big round plastic ball that the mother can use in numerous ways, including sitting on, squatting on, resting on, and supporting her body during contractions. A doula may also bring hot and cold packs with her and know massage techniques such as where to apply counter-pressure during contractions.

FACT

Surveys indicate that physicians deliver about 85 percent of all babies, while midwives oversee about 10 percent of all births. Doulas are present for roughly 5 percent of all babies born. Couples generally give high marks to their physicians as well as midwives, with the doulas also receiving high quality ratings for support given to the mother during labor.

How the Doula Supports You

Even if a member of your partner's family will be in the room with you, you still may want to hire a doula. At the same time, you may be thinking, "Heck, why do I need to pay someone to do stuff I can do myself?" Many men also worry that a doula will take over their job.

The truth is, you are going to get tired and possibly frustrated, and a doula may be able to employ methods and techniques of moving the labor along that you are not aware of. She is a woman, probably a mom, and she knows what your partner is going through. She is also a nonmedical person with experience you can confide in. The doula will be an assistant to your partner and you, not someone who is there to run the show.

You may need to take a break from time to time but not want to leave your partner alone. You may have had to leave your car in emergency parking and, after checking your partner into the hospital, you may not have even had five minutes to go back downstairs and move your car to the overnight hospital parking lot where it belongs. Having a doula (or family member, or both) assisting in the birth gives you more freedom and flexibility and takes some of the weight off your shoulders.

A birth coach has a lot of responsibility. He is his partner's greatest cheerleader and her chief advocate at the hospital. He must support her physically and emotionally. He must sometimes make decisions on her behalf as well as his unborn child's. With everything that is going on, you may want to enlist a family member or hire a trained labor assistant to help make the birth experience as smooth as possible.

CHAPTER 15

The Big Day Arrives

It is here! The big day has finally arrived, the day that you have been planning for and thinking about for months. In these pages you will find out what to do when your partner goes into labor, and the countdown to your baby begins.

Getting Labor Started

In many pregnancies, especially first ones, there comes a time when you think the baby is never going to arrive. In the heady early days, perhaps, the pregnancy sped along quickly. Around the eighth or ninth month, though, the wait for baby seems to slow down. It's like watching grass grow.

The due date comes and goes, and still there is no baby. The anticipation is hard on you, but it is much harder on your partner. They gave her a going-away party at work, but that was weeks ago. Since then she has been knocking around the house, trying to think about something other than the baby. It's been impossible.

She's been tired, more tired than ever. She doesn't even want to go outside anymore, what with total strangers coming up to her at the market and feeling her belly. "When is the bun coming out of the oven?" they ask her, thinking they're making a joke. Meanwhile, her family has cranked up the pressure by calling the house and asking if anything has happened yet.

FACT

It is becoming more common for couples to artificially induce labor. In one study, 53 percent of women used artificial oxytocin, usually given through an intravenous drip, as a means of stimulating or increasing labor contractions. In this study, this procedure induced labor in 80 percent of the women who used it.

People do a variety of things to try to jump-start those contractions on their own. Some people believe that intercourse can make a woman go into labor. In normal pregnancies this is not true, but you may have some fun while you're trying. Some pregnant women also take capsules of evening primrose oil as a means of readying the cervix and possibly stimulating labor. Evening primrose oil is available at markets and pharmacies, but again, there is no scientific evidence to support these claims.

Some people also believe that a full moon or an incoming tide, or a convergence of both, can cause labor. Sorry—that's just superstition. The fact is, you're on baby time now. Unless you choose to induce labor through drugs (or proceed with a Cesarean birth as discussed in Chapter 17), you are going to have to wait until the baby decides she is ready. Sometimes even labor-inducing drugs do not induce the baby to come.

The Stages of Labor

If you go by what you see on television or in the movies, labor takes about five minutes. First the woman feels something, and then the couple is madly racing to the hospital. Then you see the woman grunting and pushing and the baby pops out. Just like that.

For normal first-time pregnancies, it almost never goes so quickly or smoothly. Second pregnancies are different; those labors can go relatively quickly. But if this is your partner's first, count on it taking a long time— eight, twelve, eighteen, twenty-four hours or more.

Early Labor

Many people liken labor and delivery to a marathon race. This is an apt comparison because both go on for a long time and all of the participants need to be prepared to go the distance. Mom needs to keep her fluid levels up just like a marathon runner, and she and her coach both need to preserve their strength so they make it all the way.

Early labor is the beginning stage of the marathon. It can last for many hours and can begin early in the afternoon and continue through the night. Much, if not all, of early labor will likely occur while you are still at home.

How do you know when early labor begins? The surest sign is that your partner's contractions begin to occur at regular intervals, less than ten minutes apart. She will probably notice this over a period of time and mention it to you. Her contractions will gradually become stronger, longer, and occur more frequently.

Active Labor

Active labor is the second major phase in the process. It usually occurs over a shorter time span than early labor. It may last only a couple of hours, although it may seem like an eternity to your partner. Typically, you head to the hospital early in the active labor stage.

During labor, the woman's cervix gradually opens, or "dilates," and thins out, or "effaces." Her cervix must be completely effaced and dilated to ten centimeters before she can begin to push the baby out and, ultimately, give birth. Her contractions are the means her body uses to dilate and efface her cervix and move the baby toward birth.

In early labor, contractions can last thirty to forty-five seconds or sometimes less. They are milder and not as strong as what will come later, and some women may not even notice them for a while. Active labor is when the contractions get kicked up a notch. They last up to a minute or so in this stage, and your partner will definitely feel them, big-time.

Early labor may dilate your partner's cervix up to three centimeters, and active labor will bring it to around six or seven. Such considerations—how far your partner is effaced and how many centimeters she is dilated—will seem like abstractions to you until you get involved in the labor. You will quickly realize their importance, though. The two of you are trying to reach a goal, and those numbers will tell you how close you are to getting there.

Transition

Transition is the next big phase of labor, and it is the wildest and most intense by far. Everything kicks into hyper-drive. The contractions last sixty to ninety seconds and are very intense, with the woman climbing Himalayan peaks of pain. Contractions take place every two to three minutes. Your partner will barely get a chance to recover from the last wave before another one, perhaps of greater intensity, washes over her.

ALERT

If a laboring mother pushes too soon, it can slow down delivery. One of your jobs is to help her fight the urge to push. Tell her to blow or pant with her breath. Help her remember any breathing techniques she may have learned. Slow, even breaths between contractions may relax her.

Transition can last anywhere from fifteen minutes to an hour and is like the sprint to the finish line. It is during transition that the cervix reaches the promised land of ten centimeters, allowing the woman to push.

Pushing

Next comes pushing, which will be discussed in greater detail in Chapter 16. Unlike what you see in the movies or on television, pushing is not a matter of a couple quick grunts and you're done. It can last up to an hour and a half or more. When it's time to push, you—and especially your partner—still have a lot of work left to do.

Even so, most laboring Moms welcome the chance to push. Although it is still painful and they are utterly exhausted by this time, being able to push gives them a sense of control that they lacked during transition and earlier in the labor. At long last, they get to assert themselves and do something to birth their baby.

Early Signs of Progress

Early in the pregnancy, your partner experienced what are called Braxton Hicks contractions. These are sort of practice contractions that slowly get her body ready to deliver the baby. As the due date nears, these contractions can become more frequent and sometimes painful, but they are usually only a warm-up act for the real thing. One of the surest signs of real labor—as opposed to "false labor" or, more accurately, prelabor—is that your partner's contractions become regular.

There are other signs that labor may be beginning. One is called "the bloody show." This is when the mucous plug, which acts like a cork in the cervix, gets discharged, accompanied by some blood. Your partner will almost certainly tell you when this occurs. If you are at work, you may receive a phone call telling you to come home or at least be prepared for action.

The bloody show, however, does not necessarily mean that labor is imminent. It could be, of course, but it is impossible to say for sure. After the mucous plug comes unglued, a day or two can sometimes pass before the woman starts her labor.

A clearer sign that labor is on the way is when your partner's "water" or "bag of waters" breaks. The amniotic sac that protects the fetus has broken, and labor (if it hasn't started already) will probably occur within twelve to twenty-four hours or possibly sooner. Sometimes a woman's water can break while she is asleep in the middle of the night and can be quite painful and shocking. Some may experience it as a slight trickle of fluids that they need to investigate.

Once the water breaks, most physicians want labor to begin within twenty-four hours. If it has not, they will use prostaglandin gel on the cervix or other means to stimulate the start of labor. The water has served as a barrier to possible infection, and the baby cannot safely stay in the womb too long without that protection.

But again, there are many variations. Some women experience labor contractions for hours and hours before their water breaks. With others, their water breaks but they do not begin contractions for a day or more. When a medical practitioner induces labor, one of the steps she may take is to artificially rupture the membranes.

Keeping Early Labor Moving Along

Once labor begins for real, you want to make steady progress toward your goal. While the pain will never be easy for your partner to endure, she will feel better if she sees that her contractions are producing results—that is, if her cervix is continuing to dilate and efface. It is frustrating for you both when labor stalls, and all the hard work she is doing appears to be achieving nothing.

This is where you, as labor coach, can play a valuable role. During early labor, when the two of you are at home, there are some things you can do to help keep things moving along, such as:

- Take a gentle walk with her.
- Encourage her to sit up. (Lying down will slow labor.)
- Prepare a bath for her (if her water hasn't broken yet) or a shower.
- Massage her shoulders or back.
- Bring out the birthing ball and let her lean her body across it while she is having a contraction.
- Find ways to help her relax and distract her mind by playing cards or a board game or watching a movie.

Rest and relaxation are essential for both of you. You probably have a long way to go before the baby is born, so pace yourselves. Though you both want to make progress, it is important that you remain a calming influence on your partner. Encourage her. Tell her what a great job she is doing. Putting pressure on her will only cause her to tense up, and this will delay progress.

ESSENTIAL

One of your jobs will be to time your partner's contractions. Use a wristwatch or the stopwatch on your cell. The timing starts from the beginning of one contraction and extends to the beginning of the next, including the rest period in between. You will probably go to the hospital when you see that her contractions are occurring about five minutes apart or less.

Things You Need to Do

It is likely that at some point during the pregnancy, and possibly at a number of other times as well, you have felt like a fifth wheel, useless and basically irrelevant to the grand pageant unfolding within your partner's body. You may have wondered why everyone makes such a big fuss over men getting involved in childbirth when there seems to be so little for them to do.

You're not alone if you've had these thoughts; lots of men have them. But at that moment when your partner goes into labor—the real thing—all your feelings of being unneeded or unwanted disappear in a heartbeat. There are suddenly lots of things to do, and you are just the person to do them.

Stay Calm

Your partner is going through something she has never gone through before. She has no idea what she is about to experience. It's natural that she may feel a rush of emotions—happiness, relief, fear, anxiety—when labor finally kicks in. Adding to these feelings will be the pain that wracks her body every time a contraction comes on.

You will also feel a variety of emotions. You are going to be excited and happy and relieved as well. At long last, things are finally happening. You may have gotten a call from your partner to come home from work. You may have already been at home, watching a movie together, when the contractions started. Her labor may have started in the middle of the night, waking you from a sound sleep.

QUOTE

With all the emotions of going into labor, it is easy to for Dads and Moms to want to suddenly jump in the car and head off for the hospital. Not so fast, says Laurie Chamberlain, a mother of two who teaches childbirth classes. "The biggest mistake most first-time parents make is to get to the hospital too early," she says. "Remember this: head to the hospital when contractions are 4 minutes apart, 1 minute long, for 1 hour, or 411." Once that happens, then you can hit the road.

Whatever your specific situation, the operating rule at this point is simple: be cool and calm. Depending on who she is and how she responds to the pain, your partner may be having a rough time. You can best serve her by being someone she can lean on, both physically and emotionally. You need to be strong and solid and deliver for your partner in the clutch.

The Importance of Rest

Whatever the time of day your partner's contractions started, you can almost count on her to be laboring well into the night. There is a theory that the reason so many women labor at night dates back to prehistoric times. When they gave birth, cave women needed a safe, secure place in which they could feel protected. At night, under cover of darkness, they were less exposed to potential danger. You may laugh at this theory, but it is pretty much a sure bet that you will lose at least one night of sleep during labor.

Because labor can last so long, and because it often extends overnight, rest is very important. Your partner needs to rest and relax as much as possible between contractions. As crazy as it may sound, she may need to go back to bed to see if she can sleep. She will soon need all the strength and energy she can muster.

This is true for you, too. You need to pace yourself and try to rest, even if the contractions are occurring during the day. Remember that labor is like running a marathon; it's a long, grueling ordeal, and you want to be as alert as possible all the way to the end.

Use Your Nervous Energy

Realistically, though, when your partner goes into contractions, you will be excited and have lots of nervous energy at first. While remaining calm and cool, channel that nervous energy into doing all the things you need to do to get ready to go to the hospital. These tasks include:

- Calling the hospital to let them know what is going on.
- Calling anyone—family member, doula—who may be assisting you in the labor.
- Fixing a lunch and snacks for yourself (and snacks for your partner).
- Helping your partner pack her stuff if she needs assistance.
- Gathering up what you need—charged-up cell phone, toothbrush, birth aids, overnight bag, camera, camcorder.
- Packing the car.
- Making sure the car seat is installed.

Take care of these things as soon as you can after your partner goes into early labor and her contractions become regular. With these tasks out of the way, you can better focus on assisting her. You will also have some peace of mind, knowing that when it is time to go to the hospital, you will be ready.

Be a Team Player

It is possible that while you're running around doing all these things to be helpful, your feelings may get hurt. Your partner may say something that doesn't seem appreciative of all that you have done and are doing for her. Later on at the hospital the nurses and doctors may ignore you as they focus their attention on her.

This is the way it goes when you're a labor coach. It's not exactly a thankless job, because your partner appreciates what you're doing even though she may not be able to say so in the moment. Her family certainly appreciates you as well. But your needs, at this time, are secondary. In other words, you've got to check your ego at the door.

Be a team player. In this case, that means serving your partner. Your job is to help her with whatever she needs in the moment. Do that, and you will receive all the thanks you will ever need when you hold your baby in your arms.

The Best Place for Early Labor

When a pregnant woman goes into labor in the movies or on television, everybody immediately jumps up and rushes to the hospital. In most first labors, however, you will generally have time to assess the situation for a while before you have to take action.

Remember that you do not want to go to the hospital too early. You will be sent back home if you arrive too soon and your partner's cervix is not adequately effaced and dilated. A high percentage of people having their first baby must make more than one trip to the hospital before giving birth. As disappointing as this can be, it is sometimes not such a bad thing since home is a better place to spend early labor.

ALERT

The nurses are at the hospital. They cannot see your partner; they are relying on you to tell them what is going on. You and your partner are the best judges of what needs to be done at home. If you feel the situation warrants it, tell them you're coming in and want to be seen at the hospital.

Often what happens when you arrive at a hospital, even if they admit you, is that your partner's contractions slow down. Though many hospitals have tried hard to make labor and delivery rooms more comfortable, they are still far less cozy than your own home. Whether she is conscious of doing this or not, your partner will probably tense up in this new and unfamiliar environment. The tension she feels will then slow down her progress.

Stay in touch with the hospital. Tell them what is going on—the interval between your partner's contractions, whether or not she has ruptured her bag of waters, how long she has been laboring, and how well she is coping. The nurses there will be your best guide.

The Drive to the Hospital

Driving your partner to the hospital is one of the most important things you will do as her labor coach. It is anything but routine to be behind the wheel of a car while the person in the seat next to you is groaning with pain. You want to be attentive to her, and yet you have to keep your eyes on the road.

Here, again, Hollywood sets a bad example. Inevitably, in the movies and television, the ride to the hospital is a wild, high-speed dash in which the driver runs through red lights, knocks over fire hydrants, and terrorizes pedestrians. This is probably not a wise approach for you.

Although you will naturally want to get to the hospital as quickly as you can, go light on the accelerator pedal. This is not the Daytona 500. Don't run any red lights. Pay attention to the speed limit, and keep the ride smooth. A rough ride will only increase your partner's tension and pain, not ease it.

Women in labor sometimes do give birth on the way to the hospital, but these women are nearly always experiencing their second or third or fourth labors, not their first. If this is your first it is a good bet that, under normal circumstances, you will make it to the hospital in plenty of time.

Before you take off, make sure your partner has her seat belt on. The strap across her abdomen may be awkward and uncomfortable, but she still needs to put it on. If you have to brake suddenly or you're hit by somebody, she and your child need to be safe.

Studies have shown that accidents occur more frequently when people are distracted and have more than one thing on their mind. Stress can also cause people to try to handle too many things at once. When people narrow their focus and eliminate distractions, the accident rate decreases measurably.

The advice to drive safely may seem obvious and routine, but what sometimes happens to people in stressful situations is that they forget the obvious and act a little crazy. This includes fathers-to-be when they're driving their partners to the hospital.

It is exciting when labor finally starts for real. It is also a great relief. You have helped comfort your partner during early labor, taking walks with her, giving her the support she needs, timing her contractions, calling the hospital, and informing the rest of the birth team. You have packed the car and are on your way to the hospital. The time is fast approaching when you will finally meet your baby.

CHAPTER 16

Labor and Delivery

Helping deliver your child is unlike anything you will experience in your life. Your partner is going to work hard and endure incredible pain, and you are going to be with her the whole way. At the end, the two of you will have a baby. This chapter explains what you can expect and how to get through it.

Checking In

The first thing you need to understand about having a baby is that, although it may be a new experience for you and your partner, your local hospital or birthing center delivers babies all the time. They deliver dozens of babies every week, hundreds of babies every month, and thousands over the course of a year. It is anything but a novel experience for the hospital.

As such, you are going to be subject to certain routine check-in procedures when you arrive with your partner, be it in the middle of the night or in the midst of active labor. She may be suffering contractions and groaning in pain, but you will still have to produce her medical insurance card, answer questions, fill out forms, and follow whatever procedures your hospital requires. They will not immediately rush your partner into the birthing room the way they do in the movies.

As discussed earlier, childbirth preparation classes usually include a hospital tour. If you attended these classes, you probably already know the general layout of the hospital—where to park your car, where the maternity wing is, how to get there. It is helpful to check out things ahead of time because you really don't want to be wandering around the halls of the hospital asking people for directions while your partner is groaning in agony next to you.

ESSENTIAL

Patience is the rule when you check into the hospital on the night of the birth. It is going to take time, much longer than you expected. There will be delays. You and your partner will likely sit in the room a while. Staying relaxed and calm may help your partner do the same.

The admitting room is where your partner must stop and be checked out before the nurses will let her into a room. She will be asked to undress and slip into a hospital gown. Her blood pressure, temperature, and pulse will be checked. Two monitoring belts will be wrapped around her belly—one to measure the fetal heartbeat, the other to gauge the strength and duration of her contractions. These measurements will be recorded on a display monitor and printed out on graph-like paper.

A doctor will give your partner a vaginal exam to determine how far her cervix is effaced and dilated. These terms are foreign to most guys at first, but by the end of the evening you will be an expert on them. Hospital procedures vary, but a woman will normally not be admitted until she is dilated to four centimeters.

Being Sent Home

One of the most frustrating things that can happen is for a couple to arrive at the hospital thinking that the woman is about to give birth and then, when doctors determine that her cervix is not sufficiently dilated and she is not ready to give birth, be sent home again. Your partner may cry tears of disappointment if this happens. You may be angry and confused. Unfortunately, there is really nothing to do other than accept the doctor's judgment and return home.

Your partner's cervix must be dilated ten centimeters in order to begin the pushing that precedes birth. If she is dilated less than four centimeters or so, her body is not yet close enough to giving birth and you won't be admitted. She needs to labor more. Even if your partner is having frequent contractions, she may be sent home if she is not dilated adequately.

As disappointing as this is, it sometimes truly is the best thing. At home, your partner will feel more relaxed, and she may make more progress than if she had stayed at the hospital. Here are some things you can do if you have to return home:

- Let her express her disappointment at coming back home.
- Reassure her and encourage her that she is close to the four-centimeter mark and she will get there.
- Continue to walk gently with her to keep the labor moving along.
- Use your breathing techniques, the birthing ball, or other methods you have learned to help her manage the pain.
- Help her into the shower and let the hot water cascade off her back.
- Maintain a positive frame of mind, and keep encouraging her so she does the same.
- Drink water.
- Rest, rest, rest. (You both will need it.)

Rest for you both is vital, and yet you also want the labor to progress. Keep timing those contractions. You may have to go home for an hour or two, possibly spend the night, or be there for as long as a day. Stay in touch with the hospital. The nurses will advise you on when you can come in again, based on the specifics of your situation.

ESSENTIAL

The nurses will be your main point of contact with the hospital staff, but that does not mean they will be spending every moment with you and your partner. They have other laboring women to attend to. There may be one or more shift changes while you are there. The nurse you begin labor with may not be the same one you finish with.

Birthing Room Procedures

Once your partner reaches the magic threshold of four centimeters or there-abouts, she will be admitted into a birthing room. Because you were generous enough to give up Monday Night Football one evening and go down to the hospital to take the tour with your partner, you have already seen this room or one like it. This is where you will spend the next several hours until your baby is born.

Activity of Nurses

When you check into your birthing room, a nurse (or nurse-midwife) will be assigned to your partner. She will have read the birth plan you brought with you and be familiar with your specific needs and desires for the birth.

She will ask your partner questions about the labor as well as her pregnancy history. She will want to know if your partner has experienced the bloody show or if her water is still intact. She may talk to you briefly about pain medication, referring you to the attending physician or the anesthesiologist, both of whom will appear at some point to introduce themselves.

In most labor and delivery situations, you are going to interact more with the nurses than the doctors. The attending physician may make an appearance during labor but not show up again until the moment of birth, when she is there to catch the baby. The anesthesiologist will give your partner an epidural—if your partner so desires—and, under normal circumstances, this may be the last you see of him.

Additionally, the nurse may only stay a few minutes when she checks up on you. She and her colleagues may go in and out of your room. Later, as the labor gains momentum and moves into the "rock 'em, sock 'em" transition phase, the nurse will be a constant presence and a source of strength.

The Labor and Delivery Room

The center of the labor and delivery room is your partner's bed. This is where she will be and where nearly all the action will take place. There will likely be a shower in your room, some labor and delivery rooms also have birthing tubs. Furnishings might include a large chair that folds into a bed, where you can sleep if the labor lasts overnight and you need to rest.

Your partner will again be hooked up to the external monitoring belts that were used in the admitting room. In high-risk pregnancies, or when the baby is having problems, the doctor may also decide to connect her to an internal fetal monitor. In this procedure, an electrode is inserted through the woman's cervix and placed on the baby's scalp. This kind of internal monitoring is used because it supplies more precise measurements than external means.

FACT

Many women express the desire to have a "natural childbirth," but the phrase means different things to people. Most women today use pain-killers of some sort, such as Advil. Furthermore, most expect some level of technological intervention when giving birth. Surveys have shown that nearly all women use electronic fetal monitoring. The majority of women use an intravenous drip.

Before the labor gets too intense, your partner may be set up for an intra-venous drip, although the actual drip may not begin until later. She will likely receive a saline solution through the IV to replenish the fluids she is losing due to her extreme exertion. The nurses may use the IV as well to give her pain-killing drugs and oxytocin (such as Pitocin) to induce or speed labor along, if needed.

The Birth Team

Childbirth has traditionally been seen as a female process, undertaken and supervised by women with little or no involvement from men. Nowadays, women are still the dominant players, but it is no longer their exclusive domain. Most births in the United States take place in hospitals, with both male and female physicians and nurses participating. Then, of course, there is dear old Dad doing his job as labor coach.

Ideally, having a baby is a team effort. You and your partner have assembled a team to help you deliver your child. The goal of every member of the team is the same: a healthy and safe delivery for both mother and child.

The Nonmedical Team

Every birth team has two sides: the medical and the nonmedical. As birth coach, you are the captain of the nonmedical side. Your main job is to assist your partner in any way she needs it. You do what needs to be done, and you make decisions after listening to what the other members of your team say.

If you chose to recruit some help from a family member or a doula, this person (or persons) is also part of the nonmedical side of your team. She is there so that the entire burden of helping your partner does not fall entirely on you.

The Medical Side

The medical side of your team consists of the nurse-midwife, the nurses, the physician on-call, the anesthesiologist, and other medical aides who may assist during the birth. They are the trained professionals. They have birthed babies countless times before, and you will rely on their expertise and experience to do it yet again.

As your partner's chief advocate and the father of the child, you have a voice in what goes on in the labor and delivery room. Ultimately, however, the nurses and doctors are in charge. They have the final say on matters related to the health and safety of your partner and child.

Possible Friction Between the Sides

You may be saying to yourself, "Well, of course, the doctors are going to have the final word, and thank God for that. I'm not trained to make medical decisions." But it's slightly more complicated than that. When the issue is clear-cut—for example, if the baby is in extreme distress and an emergency Cesarean section must be performed—the medical staff will act quickly and decisively. Chapter 17 discusses the unexpected things that can happen during childbirth in greater detail.

ALERT

Communication is vital during labor and delivery. Keep your partner posted on what you're doing. If you have to leave the room, remember to tell her before you go. If you have to leave the building to park the car or for any other reason, be sure to tell the nurses where you are and how soon you will be back.

In many normal labor and delivery situations, however, the right thing to do is not precisely clear in that moment. At some point, the nurses may suggest pain medication to help your partner, but she may not yet be emotionally ready to accept that. She may want to keep working and laboring a while longer to see if she can make more progress before using drugs.

Neither side—your partner's or the nurse's—is right or wrong; they're just different approaches. In the end, your partner may accept medication. In figuring out what works for you, you may occasionally encounter some friction or a disagreement with the hospital staff. Remember that you're all on the same team, working toward the same goal.

When Labor Stalls

To be admitted to the hospital in a normal delivery, your wife has to be dilated to close to four centimeters or less than halfway up the mountain you need to climb. The two of you still have a lot of work to do. Her cervix needs to dilate six more centimeters and become 100-percent effaced before your baby can be born.

It may take many hours to reach the four-centimeter mark. You may have driven to the hospital, been turned away, and had to go back home. Finally, after many more arduous and painful contractions, you and your partner are admitted to the birthing room. After making it this far, it is natural to think the rest is going to be easy.

It is always possible, of course, that this next phase will go smoothly and that your partner will make solid, steady progress. It is also possible that the labor will stall at some point. Your partner will continue having regular and frequent contractions, but they will not bring her any closer to the top of the mountain—again, to that all-important ten centimeter mark.

ESSENTIAL

Sometimes nurses do not pay as much attention to your partner as you would like. If your labor has stalled, you may need to find your nurse and request that she become more actively engaged. Her energy and knowledge may give you and your partner the boost you need.

For example, she could jump from four to six centimeters relatively quickly. Then an hour or so could pass, filled with hard contractions. Your nurse could then return and do another check but this time deliver the bad news that you're still at six—no progress. It's discouraging.

What do you do then? Encourage your partner; help her shift into different positions to stimulate the labor. Get her up and walking, if she can. Give her ice chips for thirst and make sure she is comfortable. Continue to use the breathing and other birthing techniques you've learned, and keep plugging away.

Pain Relief Options

Labor and delivery is not a masochism contest. The point of it is not to see how much pain your partner can withstand before she cries "Uncle!" Pain medication is a valid and widely used option for women in labor.

For many men, it is difficult to see the women they love in so much pain. It is far more difficult, of course, for the woman to suffer through this pain. Drugs can provide relief for her.

Epidural

Many women who have had babies like to joke that the sexiest man they have ever met is the anesthesiologist who gave them an epidural during labor. Before the anesthesiologist entered the picture, these women were suffering mightily. After he left, they felt much, much better. Some women, it is said, even name their babies after their anesthesiologists.

An epidural block, as it is formally called, is safe and easy to administer through an injection in the spine. One big reason that women like it—apart from the fact that it takes them out of pain—is that they can remain awake during labor. The pain relief extends to the lower part of the body, leaving the head clear. When the woman's child is born, she can welcome her with open arms and an alert mind.

Many couples decide in advance that they want to have an epidural and include it in their birth plans. Even so, this doesn't leave them entirely off the hook. Getting an epidural too early in the process can slow down her delivery. That means you both are going to have to work and labor for a while to reach the point at which the medication can achieve the best results.

Analgesics

Narcotic analgesics are another form of pain medication used in labor and delivery. Demerol, fentanyl, and other powerful pain relievers are usually administered intravenously. While they do offer pain relief, they are not as popular as epidurals because they can affect a woman's ability to think clearly and be present in the moment. Furthermore, many women report panicky feelings while on these drugs, making them less able to handle the pain they are experiencing.

ALERT

Do not allow analgesics to be given to your partner too close to the time of delivery. These drugs can make your newborn drowsy and unresponsive, affecting her breathing and heart rate. The baby can be treated successfully in most cases with oxygen and by other means, but the risks are higher with analgesics than with epidurals.

If you and your partner originally wanted to do a "natural" delivery, without the use of an epidural or other drugs, circumstances may force you to change your mind. Your partner may be in so much pain, and making so little progress, that you feel you have no other choice. Before you make the final call, though, give yourself some time to think about it. During that period, you might make enough progress that the drugs are no longer warranted. An epidural, however, can only be administered at a certain stage in the labor, so you can't wait too long before you make this decision.

Pushing

Pushing may be the best time in all of labor. Your partner has worked her way through early and active labor. She has survived the horror-show known as transition, which has opened her cervix from about seven centimeters to ten. Having arrived there, she can finally push. Being able to push her baby out, to exert herself in this way, often gives a woman a renewed sense of power and energy.

It's a good time for you, too. You've traveled this long road with her. You've been there the whole way, and the end appears to be in sight. Unlike in the movies, though, pushing seldom ever takes only a few minutes. It can last anywhere from thirty minutes to two hours or longer.

With your partner pushing and becoming more physically assertive, her legs are spread wide and she is back on her buttocks. You will probably be holding one of her legs, while a nurse is holding the other. Both of you intently watch the monitor to see when the next contraction is coming on. She can push when a contraction comes on. She grits her teeth and summons all her energy while you encourage her and tell her to give it everything she has.

After the contraction passes, she relaxes. Then another contraction comes up and she makes another supreme effort. And another and another. During the contractions, her voice rises to a scream, but you tell her that her cries only disperse her energy. She needs to direct her power downward with a low, guttural growl.

Down and out, that's your message to your partner. Down and out. Then your baby's head appears for the first time in the birth canal.

Congratulations! You're a Father!

By this time, the on-call doctor has arrived to catch the baby. The room is a beehive of activity. There are several nurses in the room, preparing sterile instruments in case they are needed and getting things ready for when the baby emerges. A mirror has been placed in such a way to allow your partner to see the baby, if she wishes.

The baby's head comes forward, then back. Forward, then back. This is called "crowning." More pushing is required, more straining, more grunting. Then comes one last push, and there he is.

QUOTE

"When Luke was born," said late newscaster Tim Russert about the birth of his child, "I suddenly understood the meaning of unconditional love." So will you. It sounds corny, but the emotions you feel when you help bring a new life into the world will be unlike anything you've ever felt before.

First Impressions

You may fall rapturously in love with your child on first sight, as many parents do. Then again, you may feel a mix of emotions, in part because your child looks, well, odd. His wrinkly skin may look discolored and his head may be slightly misshapen, like he is a member of the Conehead family. Both of these conditions will go away with time, so you can relax. Your child's skin tones will gradually look the way they should. The Conehead effect, which is caused by his recent journey down the narrow birth canal, will also diminish, and his head will be an ordinary shape.

Cutting the Cord

Many men choose to cut their child's umbilical cord. It is a simple, safe, and easy procedure. The cord is clamped off on either side by the medical staff, leaving you a small area to snip with a pair of scissors that they give you. Don't worry; you won't slip.

The act of cutting the cord has grown in popularity in recent years. It is another way in which men can be involved in the act of childbirth. There is a symbolic aspect to it; the father is the one who severs the physical connection between mother and child. If it is not something that appeals to you, however, all you have to do is politely say no.

Another recent trend is to store, or "bank," your child's umbilical cord blood. Cord blood is a rich source of stem cells, and if your child or a family member developed cancer or a blood disease later in life, these stem cells could potentially be used in treatment.

Holding the Baby

Virtually all mothers are going to want to hold their babies and have skin-to-skin contact with them as soon after birth as possible. This is right and proper. Mom did all the work (or most of it); she gets first dibs. Almost immediately, the nurses or your doula will help show her how to breastfeed her baby.

After Mom, though, it's your turn. Don't be shy; give it a whirl. Before they become fathers, lots of guys are not quite sure about holding a baby. It's like a baby is some sort of rare and expensive antique vase. They fear they'll drop him or hold him wrong and somehow hurt him.

Once you become a father, these fears disappear. He's your son; of course you're going to pick him up and hold him. You've never met him before, and you're only starting to get to know him, but you have been through a lot together already, and you have formed a relationship. And your relationship is only beginning.

The Afterbirth

So the baby has entered the world. She's healthy, and you're bonding up a storm with her. Okay, time to pack it up and go home, right? No, not quite. There is still another job to do: birthing the afterbirth.

The afterbirth, or placenta, has sustained your child while inside the womb, feeding and supporting her. Its job is done, and it cannot remain inside your partner's body. It has to come out the same way the baby did: traveling down the birth canal.

Birthing the placenta can take anywhere from five to twenty-five minutes or more. Your partner will continue to have contractions (though milder than before), which means that you've got to help her get through them. In other words, you're back on the job, Coach. Give your child to a nurse, and turn your attention back to your partner, encouraging her and helping her to finish this one last job. When she's done, you're done.

ESSENTIAL

Every woman is different, and so is every labor. Your job as labor coach is to dial into what is going on with your partner and respond to what she needs, based on the situation at hand. Be pro-active. Rather than waiting for her to tell you what to do, make a suggestion and give it a try.

Be aware, too, that your partner may need to be stitched up after birth. The perineum is the skin on the bottom side of the vaginal opening. She may have had an episiotomy or incision to prevent bad tearing in this area, or she may have torn from the exertion of labor. This will be an uncomfortable several minutes for her.

And so you and your partner have made your journey. You checked into the hospital as a couple and then, with the birth team assembled around your partner and working as a unit, the most amazing and mind-blowing event of your life occurred: your baby was born. You will leave the hospital as a family.

CHAPTER 17

Real-Life Birth Scenarios

The Boy Scout motto of "Be prepared!" is an excellent rule for expectant fathers and mothers, but sometimes things happen when you're having a baby that you're not prepared for. In fact, you can almost count on it. This chapter tells you about some of the unexpected things that can happen and how to get ready for them.

Expect the Unexpected

Like most pregnant couples these days, you will prepare a birth plan explaining how you would like the labor and delivery to proceed—whether or not your partner wants to have an epidural or other pain medication, whether she wants to be connected to an IV drip or have electronic fetal monitoring during labor, what the atmosphere of the birthing room should be like, and so forth.

Many pregnant couples (particularly the mom-to-be) spend a great deal of time thinking about and writing their plan. Some are quite detailed and specific, with precise instructions to the medical staff on a number of issues related to the birth. No matter how detailed your plan is, however, you can never predict what will happen during your child's birth. Almost assuredly, something is going to occur that you did not expect and did not plan for.

ESSENTIAL

Talk about contingency plans with your partner and figure out some "What will we do if" scenarios. She may have strong ideas about the birth and be unwilling to talk about alternatives. Affirm what she wants, but gently try to come up with a Plan B and even a Plan C. You may not need to use these backup plans, but it is good to be prepared.

Flexibility Is the Key

How do you prepare for the unexpected? You do all the things you're doing now: you read about pregnancy, talk to your partner, talk to other people who have had kids, and go to childbirth classes. While none of this will specifically instruct you on how to handle an abrupt change in plans, it will give you a solid grasp of what occurs during labor and delivery and help you deal with whatever comes up.

You will need to be flexible. So will your partner. Although you may have put a lot of time and care into your birth plan, it is not a tablet carved in stone. You will be better off if you approach labor and delivery with the idea that unexpected events can occur, and that these events may cause you to change your plans.

Premature Birth

A full-term pregnancy is defined as one that reaches anywhere from thirty-seven-to forty-two weeks. A birth is premature when the baby is born earlier than thirty-seven weeks. If you are expecting twins, there is a high probability that your bundles of joy will arrive before thirty-seven weeks. This means that you and your partner need to have everything in place and be ready to go to the hospital at least a couple of weeks before then.

No one can say precisely what causes many babies to be born prematurely, but medical authorities have been able to pinpoint certain risk factors of "preterm labor," as it is called. In addition to having twins or a multiple birth, those factors include:

- Drug use (including prescription drugs)
- Smoking
- Poor diet
- Drinking alcohol
- Heavy lifting or physical labor
- Obesity
- High blood pressure
- Anemia
- Not gaining enough weight during pregnancy

What is encouraging about this list is that your partner can control many of the things on it through her behavior. In other words, she can take action that reduces the risk of premature labor. Your encouragement and support may be able to help her in this regard.

Take It Seriously

Premature labor can be a very serious threat and needs to be treated as such. It is the leading cause of neonatal death, and premature babies who survive sometimes have health problems that last throughout their lives. If your partner goes into early labor, she needs to get immediate medical attention.

Depending on the pregnancy, however, having early labor contractions does not necessarily mean your partner is immediately going to give birth. Doctors sometimes tell pregnant women to go to bed and stay there as a means of preventing or delaying labor. Mothers-to-be may need to stop working or cease physical activities (including sexual intercourse). In some cases, doctors may recommend special medication or hospitalization. All of this effort should clue you into just how important it is for the baby to stay inside her mother until she reaches full term, or as close to full term as possible.

Bed Rest

Although it is more likely that your partner will be late in delivering than it is that she'll be early, you need to consider this possibility in your planning. If your partner has to leave her job early, this may force her to start drawing upon her disability and paid vacation leave sooner than she expected. This could affect your financial situation.

Premature births in the United States continue to rise. Nearly 500,000 babies a year are born premature, up substantially from previous decades. No one knows exactly why this is happening. The more widespread use of fertility drugs among couples is cited as one possible reason. Poverty and lower education levels among mothers may also contribute to this trend.

Furthermore, if the doctor orders partial or complete bed rest for your partner, you may have to do more around the house than you originally figured. Her family and friends may also have to get more involved earlier than expected. Yours, too. Everybody may need to pitch in to help bring this baby to term.

Medical Intervention

"Normal" is a term that is often used in connection with pregnancy. The expressions "under normal circumstances" and "with normal births" are common and, as you've probably noticed, they have been used frequently in this book. It is reassuring for expectant parents to know that the pregnancy is proceeding as it should and that their unborn child is developing normally.

This applies to labor and delivery as well. Parents want their child's birth to proceed normally, but there is a wide variation in what this means. One couple's "normal" may be completely different than another's. Many things can happen during labor and delivery. Medical intervention may be required if:

- The woman has back labor, causing her intense pain.
- The baby is in a "breech" position, with his buttocks rather than his head coming first down the birth canal.
- The baby stalls, requiring doctors to use forceps or suction to guide the baby out of the birth canal.
- The umbilical cord gets wrapped around the baby's neck, which may restrict blood flow.
- The cord becomes compressed, reducing or perhaps cutting off the flow of oxygen.
- The baby has his first bowel movement in the womb, causing a darkish staining (meconium).
- The baby is listless after birth, perhaps due to pain medication given to the mother.

Results are what count in the labor and delivery business, but these and many other complications can happen. Some may require immediate treatment by the nurses and doctors. Just know that you can have a wild, wild birth and still end up with a healthy, happy, normal baby.

FACT

Forceps were invented by a sixteenth-century British physician named Peter Chamberlen the elder, though the instrument didn't come into common use until the late 1800s. These tong-like instruments, used far less commonly today than in the past, grab the head of the baby in order to move him down the birth canal. The use of forceps has saved the lives of many women and children.

Baby Is Late

You can practically go to the bank on this one: if this is your partner's first baby, and everything is "normal," the child will likely be born later than her due date. This is good to know if you entered an office pool picking the day of your baby's birth.

A smart bettor would never pick the due date or any date before it. But the question remains: how many days after the due date will the baby arrive? One day? Ten days? Nobody except the baby has that information, and she's not saying.

A Frustrating Time

You've had the due date circled on your calendar for months and months. Finally, the big day arrives—and what happens? Nothing. After all that waiting, the only thing you and your partner can do now is to wait some more.

This can be a tough time for both of you. First of all, you've had your expectations dashed. Although you knew that most first births arrived late, somehow you thought yours would be different.

Another frustrated group is your family and friends. They don't like waiting any more than you do. Wisely, you did not reveal the exact due date to them, telling them only the approximate period in which the birth was supposed to occur. Even so, they know the general timetable and are starting to e-mail and call more frequently. Again, here is where some social networking might help. Post the latest news (or non-news) on your Facebook or MySpace page. People will be up-to-date on your situation, and this will maybe ease the pressure you and your partner are feeling.

Your First Lesson in Parenting

If your baby is overdue, this is actually your first lesson in parenting. You may have a timetable for your child and a certain set of expectations for her. Of course, that does not mean she is going to follow the timetable you've laid out for her or any of your expectations. What's true for teenagers and other children goes for babies just as well: they have their own agenda.

Nevertheless, you can do your best to keep things moving along. It is said that stimulating a woman's nipples may lead to contractions, but only if you do it for long hours at a time. Sexual intercourse is another fun activity to try. After the two of you are finished in bed, you might take a gentle walk together around the block.

Generally, medical authorities do not like pregnant women to go beyond the forty-two-week mark, or two weeks past the due date, over worries about the condition of the placenta. Many women are induced at that point to go into labor, although some women refuse drugs. They wait for the baby to come naturally and have successful childbirths with healthy, happy babies. You and your partner should consult with her obstetrician on the best course for her.

Other home remedies for stimulating labor include raspberry-leaf tea or evening primrose oil. None of these techniques should be attempted, however, without first consulting with a physician. Depending on where you are in the pregnancy, he may recommend oxytocin as a means of jump-starting the labor. But the best thing to do may be nothing at all—just let nature take its course.

Cesarean Delivery

The Cesarean section was named after Julius Caesar who, it was said, was born via this surgical procedure. Historians scoff at this claim, however, because using surgery to deliver a child in the days of the ancient Roman Empire was nearly certain to result in the death of the mother, and Julius's mom lived to a ripe old age. Nevertheless, the name stuck.

A Cesarean section is a surgical procedure used to deliver babies. It is a common procedure and is considered relatively safe, although it still poses some higher risks to the mother than a vaginal delivery would. Although the health risks are minor, it is nevertheless regarded as major surgery.

Cesareans are performed for a variety of reasons. The mother's pregnancy may be high-risk, and a Cesarean may be the safest way to deliver the baby. Delivering vaginally may pose problems, causing distress for the baby. The physicians may decide to get him out as quickly as possible, through surgical means. Some, though not all, doctors routinely perform Cesareans when the baby is breech—pointing his bottom, not his head, down the birth canal.

QUOTE

Chelsea Clinton, the daughter of Hillary and Bill Clinton, was born breech. In the 1970s, recalls the former President, "hospital policy did not permit fathers in the delivery room when an operation was necessary. I pleaded with the hospital administrator to let me go in." Bill's arguments won, and he was there for what he calls "the happiest moment of my life."

Unless your partner's pregnancy is considered high-risk, and she knows from the start that there is a strong likelihood of a Cesarean, she is probably not planning for one. Nearly all of the women who have had a Cesarean originally thought they were going to deliver vaginally. Circumstances can change during the course of pregnancy or labor, and it is a good idea to know a bit about them, should your partner's situation warrant it.

Coaching a Cesarean Birth

Just as few women start out their pregnancies thinking about having a Cesarean, few men consider the possibility that they may be comforting their partners not in the birthing room, but in the operating room. So the first thing is that the two of you need to at least entertain the possibility that it could happen. Have a "What if?" sort of discussion. Talk about how you want to handle a Cesarean, if it should occur, and then put those thoughts down in your birth plan.

A Cesarean is a surgical procedure, and you and your partner will have less of a voice in what goes on in the operating room than if she were going through a vaginal delivery. Nevertheless, you can state your wishes. Does your partner want to hold the baby after surgery and perhaps even try to breastfeed her while she is still on the operating table? If you've thought about these things ahead of time, and written them down in a birth plan, you will not be caught off guard when the physicians tell you that a Cesarean is necessary.

Your Place Is in the Operating Room

Some hospitals do not allow fathers-to-be with their partners in the operating room during a Cesarean. If this is the case at your hospital, ask for an exception to this policy. Except in emergencies or when general anesthesia is used and the mother is unconscious, there is no reason—medical or otherwise—why you cannot be in the room with your partner.

Talk to your partner's obstetrician, who may support you in your desire to support your partner. Explain to the powers that be that the majority of hospitals allow men in the operating room. Explain further that your partner needs you there and has requested your presence.

ALERT

It is generally agreed that many Cesareans are unnecessary. Find out what the Cesarean rate is at your hospital. If the percentage seems too high, you and your partner may want to look into having her give birth in another hospital. Some physicians may be too quick to resort to a Cesarean during a slow or more difficult labor.

The decision to have a Cesarean is sometimes made in the heat of the moment by doctors who need to extricate the baby, for the safety of both baby and Mom. If you are excluded from the operating room in an emergency, you will obviously not have time to appeal the decision. You may feel some disappointment in not being able to participate in the birth of your child, but you may be able to avoid this situation if you ask about hospital policy ahead of time.

Your Job in the Room

Since this is surgery, you will scrub your hands and arms and wear sterile hospital clothes. In the operating room, you will sit at your partner's head behind sterile drapes. The drapes will block your view of the surgery that is taking place on the lower half of your partner's body. She will receive anesthesia, which will numb her body but keep her conscious. You can hold her hand and talk to her while the surgery is taking place.

Even though a Cesarean is safe, your partner will almost certainly feel anxious and scared. She may be scared, not so much for herself but for her child, whom she cannot see. She cannot feel the lower part of her body, and she has lost control over the birth of the baby, which is now in the hands of the surgeons. Stroke your partner's forehead and softly reassure her.

When the Baby Is Born

Next comes the best news of all: your child is born. Your partner will want to hold the baby as soon as possible and, as your partner's birth coach, you should make sure she gets that opportunity. Because this is a surgical procedure, nurses and doctors follow a certain routine. Sometimes they can focus on this routine to such an extent that they overlook the urgent desire of the parents to connect with their newborn. Both you and your partner can hold the baby. If it's allowed, she may wish to try breastfeeding.

Some hospitals try to give the parents of Cesarean babies more of an intimate post-birth family experience, instead of whisking the child away immediately to the neonatal intensive care unit. Unfortunately, it will never compare to the time that parents have after a vaginal delivery. The mother in a Cesarean birth has just undergone major surgery, and she must have her abdomen stapled up. This necessity will move events along quickly.

Go with Your Child

The father's duty, at this point, is to go with his child. The surgeons need to finish up with your partner, who almost certainly will want you to stay with the baby. Again, hospital policies may dictate that your child be taken to the neonatal ICU, even though he is healthy and fine. This is another thing you can ask about when you talk to the hospital about its Cesarean policies.

If your baby is taken to the neonatal ICU, you can sit with him. You can talk to him, sing to him, and tell him how much you love him. Let him wrap him tiny fingers around one of yours.

QUOTE

For your baby, the same as for your partner, tell her frequently you love her. The Nobel Prize-winning novelist John Steinbeck, father of two sons, said, "Girls have a way of knowing or feeling what you feel, but they usually like to hear it also." This is true for sons, too.

Some hospitals will allow your newborn to be brought into the recovery room where your partner will be taken after surgery. If you can get approval for this, good for you. If not, you can be certain that after your partner is released from recovery and given a room in the maternity ward, she will be reunited with the baby and you.

Recovery from a Cesarean

Recovering from a Cesarean section is generally longer and more painful than a vaginal delivery. Not only is your partner recovering from childbirth, she has just had major surgery. Anticipate, then, that she will be facing some big physical and emotional issues in the days and weeks to come.

Physically, it is going to be tough for her to get around at first. Immediately after birth, for example, she cannot lift up the baby. The child needs to be handed to her. She will feel a certain degree of pain, although medication will ease this. After you come home, she will be on extremely limited duty. You may need to enlist recruits—family members, a paid aide—to help you out around the house.

As she recovers physically, you need to be aware that there may be emotional fallout from the Cesarean. This was not how she envisioned childbirth. She may have gripes about the physicians, feeling that they ignored her during the surgery and should have been more attentive to her feelings. She may resent the fact that she did not get to hold her newborn as much as she liked and that you got a longer chance to connect with the baby right after birth.

FACT

Cesarean deliveries continue to rise in the United States, accounting for nearly one-third of all births. Very few women request C-sections or plan to have one when they enter the hospital to give birth. Cesareans tend to occur most frequently in first births because those labors tend to last longer and are sometimes more complicated, thus requiring surgical intervention.

If your partner feels these sorts of resentments, all you can do is let her talk and then show her some sympathy. You do not want her feelings to fester. You want her to talk about them so she can let go and move ahead with her life. The birth may not have been everything she dreamed of, but you have a vibrant, healthy child, and that is what matters most of all.

CHAPTER 18

The Immediate Aftermath

Congratulations! You did it! You're a father. But your job isn't over yet. In some ways, in fact, it's only beginning. Before you can bring your partner and child home, you still have some work to do. This chapter explores the various things that come up immediately after the baby is born.

Taking a Moment with Your New Family

First things first: before you make any calls to let people know, before the relatives and friends descend on the hospital, and before all the craziness associated with having a baby begins, take a moment with just the three of you. You, your partner, your child—alone together for the first time. Ain't life grand?

At the moment of birth, the labor and delivery room was a frenzy of activity. Doctors and nurses were all over the place. Your partner was straining and pushing while you cheered her on. Then the baby was born, and shortly thereafter the nurses gave her to your partner so she could hold her and begin to learn how to breastfeed. Amidst all this, you snipped the umbilical cord and got to hold the baby yourself.

ESSENTIAL

There is an understandably anxious feeling that comes with being left alone with a newborn for the first time. If you and your partner do not feel comfortable, ask a nurse to stay in your room for a few minutes. As your confidence grows, she can leave. Ask her to check in on you again in ten minutes.

At some appropriate moment, you and your new family have a right to some peace and quiet. Ask the medical staff, the doula, and anyone else who may have assisted in the labor to leave the room because you and your partner want to be alone with the baby. It's not rude at all, and everyone will understand.

Baby Wellness Tests

Certain medical tests and procedures will be performed on your baby in the labor and delivery room. They will be done quickly and unobtrusively, either immediately after birth or shortly thereafter. The tests measure your child's health and check that his bodily systems are firing on the right cylinders.

The first test your child will receive is the Apgar. This is an acronym for the categories that the test scores: appearance, pulse, grimace (reflex), and respiration. The Apgar is administered twice—the first time at one minute after birth, and the second time at five minutes after. The child receives scores in each of the four categories, with most babies receiving a passing mark of seven to ten. Here are some other tests and procedures that the medical staff may administer:

- Suction nose to clear air passages.
- Clamp umbilical cord (after you cut it).
- Weigh and measure baby.
- Visually inspect baby, and count fingers and toes.
- Measure circumference of head.
- Apply eye drops or ointment to prevent infection.
- Give vitamin K injection to promote blood clotting.
- Draw blood from baby's heel for disease screening.
- Perform other types of blood screenings.

Depending on hospital policy, some of these tests, such as the vitamin K shot and the heel prick, may not need to be administered immediately. You may ask for them to be done a little later, allowing you and your partner to first spend some time with the baby. Another routine but essential part of a hospital birth is having identification bracelets placed on your baby, your partner, and you. Everyone wants to be sure that you take the right child home with you.

Letting Everyone Know

It is definitely Dad's job to make the calls to tell people that the baby is here and Mom is doing fine. Mom will be able to receive calls and chat on the phone once she feels rested enough to talk, but Dad is the one who typically makes the first calls to family and friends.

Not every assignment you have as a father and birth coach is fun, but this one is. After the focused intensity of the labor and delivery experience, you get to reconnect with the outside world. Although you will be tired and perhaps a little punchy, by this time you will be riding an emotional high. Your emotions will be shared by those on the other end of the line, who will be eager to hear every morsel of information you can give them.

Two Common Questions

People mainly have two questions at first: they want to know how Mom is doing, and they want to know whether it's a boy or a girl. If you have kept the name of your child a secret, this will be your first chance to break the news. Some people will want to know when they can talk to Mom, and they may even ask how you are holding up.

FACT

The average weight of a newborn is 7½ pounds, with nearly all babies tipping the scales between 5½ and 10 pounds. A newborn can lose as much as 10 percent of her body weight in her first day or two of life. The average length of a newborn is 20 inches, with most measuring somewhere between 18 and 22 inches.

When the time finally comes to make these calls, you will probably have been up all night. You might not be thinking all that clearly. This is when you can rely on that list of numbers you've put into the memory of your cell: parents (hers and yours), family members (hers and yours), close friends. You do not want to forget anyone important.

More on the Beauty of Cell Phones

A cell phone is the best communication tool you'll have, but some hospitals and birthing centers restrict the use of cells within their facilities. You need to find out what restrictions exist, if any. Even if cells are restricted, you should still be able to step outside when the time is right and make calls.

If you do not have a cell phone, you will probably end up borrowing someone else's, so it's best just to break down and buy one. If cells are permitted in the hospital, you can call from the labor and delivery room and pass the phone over to Mom if she feels like talking. If you need to leave the room to make calls, or for any other reason, check with your partner first. This could be the first time she has ever been left alone with the baby. Be sure she is comfortable and taken care of before you go.

When to Call People

Some people, usually family members who are close to Mom, will say to you, "Call me as soon as you know. I don't care if it's three o'clock in the morning. I want to know the instant the baby is born!"

In almost every case, these calls can wait until a decent hour of the morning. Do not feel obliged to make calls in the middle of the night. Wait until the morning instead. The same people who are begging for you to call will appreciate the fact that you've allowed them to get a full night's sleep, whether they admit it or not. If they give you any grief for not calling them earlier, tell them you were distracted and exhausted, which, almost assuredly, will be true.

Make It Easy on Yourself

One or two people may volunteer to be part of a phone tree to help spread the news about baby. These will likely be the same people who absolutely insist on hearing the news as soon as it happens. Their enthusiasm is a good thing, and you would do well to make use of it.

Arrange the system beforehand with them. You call them after the baby comes, and then they make some of the calls for you. Not only will this save you a little work, it is a nice gesture that lets other family members be involved. They get a chance to spread the news, which is a kick for them, too.

Other Jobs and Responsibilities

Your first responsibilities are to your partner and child. Everything else is a distant third. If you keep this in mind, you will have no trouble figuring out what needs to be done, and in what order, after the birth takes place.

Once the baby is born, the big work is done (at least while mother and child are still in the hospital). You and your partner have successfully completed your mission and can relax. But, in addition to calling friends and relatives, there are some jobs you may be called upon to perform.

Being with the Baby

You may immediately need to start looking out for the welfare of your child, even while he is still in the hospital. In a Cesarean birth, for example, the nurses will take the baby from the operating room after surgery is over. The father's responsibility is to go with his child and be with him while Mom remains behind in the doctors' hands.

In certain situations there may be fears about the child's health, and medical tests are conducted on these babies after birth. These tests are more sophisticated than the wellness checks conducted in the labor and delivery room, and they may take place in the neonatal intensive care unit. In these cases, if possible, the father should accompany the baby while Mom recovers in her room.

Gatekeeper

Your partner will naturally be excited after the birth, but she will also be exhausted. Lots of people are going to call and want to talk to her. Still more people are going to want to visit.

One of your biggest jobs will be to serve as gatekeeper. You obviously do not want to act like a bouncer at a nightclub, so just check in with your partner now and then to make sure she is handling everything okay. She won't get the rest she needs if she's entertaining visitors one after the other.

Breastfeeding Support

Breastfeeding (discussed more extensively in Chapter 19) usually begins shortly after birth. The nurse or doula places the baby on Mom's breast and begin to teach her how to do it. Despite what many men think, women do not instinctively know how to breastfeed and it can be a very difficult and painful process to learn.

FACT

The benefits of breast milk for babies are indisputable. It supplies more than 100 vitamins and nutrients that are not found in infant formula. Studies have shown that children who are breastfed tend to have higher IQs than those who are not. This is partly because of the nutrition these babies receive, but it is also because of the close interaction between mother and child, which encourages brain development.

You and your partner have probably already discussed breastfeeding. If she plans to do it (and most women do, at least initially), your encouragement and support can play a useful role in helping her to get started.

Meeting Siblings

If you have a young child, some of this information may be familiar to you because you went through it not that long ago. The age of your child (or children) will determine how you handle the news of a baby on the way. Whatever your child's age, she deserves to know about the pregnancy at a relatively early stage. She will have questions and concerns, and you need to deal with them in a thoughtful way.

Anticipate that your child's concerns will be self-centered. Her focus will be on how the baby is going to affect her. A teenager may fret about having to share her room with a new brother or sister or about not being able to spend as much time with her friends. Younger children may worry that the baby is going to replace them in your affection and that you won't have as much time to spend with them. There are numerous children's books that deal with sibling issues. Reading stories together may reassure your child and help her better understand what's coming.

When a sibling comes to meet the baby for the first time at the hospital, it is nice to have them exchange gifts. The older sibling brings a small gift for the baby, who returns the favor—thanks to your foresight in buying something ahead of time for the older child and stashing it in the bag you brought to the hospital. Younger children need a lot of leeway. They haven't seen their mothers in a couple of days, and they may be anxious about her. They will want to climb in bed with her and their new brother or sister, creating an ideal photo opportunity for you.

Taking Pictures

You are going to have your hands full during the birth and will probably not be able to stop to take pictures. Even if you do find a spare moment or two, sticking a camera in your partner's face and telling her to "Smile!" while she is in the midst of a contraction will probably not be met with a warm reception.

After the birth, though, it's a different story. Grab your camera (or camera-phone) out of your overnight bag and hand it to a nurse. Let her take a picture of your new family—Mom, Dad, baby—posed together on the hospital bed in the hour after the birth.

Dad is the main photographer especially in the hospital when Mom cannot get out of bed and is frequently holding the baby. There's nothing wrong with this; just remember to hand the camera to someone else now and then and get yourself into a picture or two. In many ways, the shots you take in the hospital will be among the most memorable you will ever have of your child. Those are the first hours and days of his life.

ESSENTIAL

With the world going digital, it is sometimes easy to forget to have your baby and family pictures printed on photographic paper the old-fashioned way. Although you can surely store photos in your computer or on CDs, it is also wise to print the best ones on paper too. Computer operating systems can go out of date, but a baby album can last for generations.

Other people will bring cameras to take pictures—the more the merrier. You can upload pictures to a photo sharing site or your Facebook page or send them around via e-mail, allowing friends, coworkers, and distant relatives a chance to see the new arrival right away.

Shooting with a Camcorder

Making a video is a wonderful thing to do as well. One advantage of moving pictures is that you are able to record sounds—the first cries and gurgles of your child as well as the laughter and chatter of the family members who come to visit.

It will likely be just fine if you bring a camcorder to the ultrasound exams or possibly other prenatal visits. Filming during the birth, however, is somewhat more questionable. You may think it's a nifty idea, but your partner may be dead-set against it. Before you get too far in your discussions, check with the hospital to see what its policy is. Some do not allow camcorders to be used during labor and delivery.

Shooting During Birth

Assuming you have the approval to go ahead with your plan to be the Steven Spielberg of baby movie production (and you're not worried about making 'Alien IV'), the best technique is to set the camcorder up on a tripod in a spot in the room that gives you a view of the bed but that is not in anyone's way. Nurses and doctors come and go during labor and delivery. This activity increases in the moments before birth. The medical people cannot be bumping into the tripod while they're trying to birth your baby.

Another reason for a tripod is that you need to have your hands free to help your partner. There may be moments where you can walk over to the camcorder and shoot some film. This will be much easier to do if it is already set up and ready to go than if you have to fumble around with it each time you want to use it.

ESSENTIAL

On this issue of filming the birth, your partner deserves veto power. If she doesn't want to be filmed during birth, that's her call to make. Even so, remember to bring the camcorder with you. Nobody will object to filming after the birth or when friends and family come to visit.

During the all-out intensity of transition and pushing, as well as the quieter, more sublime moments right after birth, you cannot adequately do your job as labor coach while doubling as director of photography. You need to concentrate on your partner and the business at hand. You may solve this problem by bringing in a friend to handle the film-making responsibilities (again, with the approval of your partner).

Celebrating the Arrival

Having a baby is a thing to celebrate. It's a unique moment in your life, and you and your partner have worked hard to reach it. With your family and closest friends around you, you deserve a good time. Relish the moment while you can.

Champagne is always good. Ask a friend to bring a bottle and some plastic glasses when he comes. Another way is flowers. The hospital gift shop may sell them.

Cigars

A traditional way for fathers to celebrate the birth of a child is with cigars. Past generations of men handed out cigars to their friends and colleagues at work, and this male-bonding tradition continues to this day. After the birth, after you bring the baby home, you and your brother or your father-in-law (or both!) can step outside on the front porch in the cool evening air, light up Macanudos, and talk.

Some cigars are sold with blue or pink cellophane wrappers that say, "It's a boy!" or "It's a girl!" These are usually less expensive cigars, and you may want to make a bolder statement with the ones you give out. Some fathers create a keepsake out of the cigar box they bought when their child was born. They store a lock of hair, photos, and other memorabilia inside.

A Gift for Mom

No one is more deserving of something special than your partner. As you will see after you go through the birth with her, this woman gave her all to bring a child of yours into the world. It is nice to recognize this in some way. A gift thanking her for her hard work, sometimes called a "push present" is a nice gesture that she will undoubtedly appreciate.

FACT

About half of all newborns stay two days in the hospital, while the other half are discharged earlier. Cesarean births can stay up to four days. Studies have shown that either one or two days in the hospital is medically acceptable, as long as there is proper follow-up care for mother and baby shortly after they go home.

You do not need to go into serious debt to buy diamond earrings or an expensive gift at this time. If you can swing it financially, that's great. But something simple and thoughtful—flowers and a card, for example—will do just fine.

You have, after all, given quite a bit of yourself as well. You've been with your partner the whole way, and now you have this beautiful, amazing, incredible baby. You were there when she needed you the most, and although it sounds corny, this was the greatest gift you could give her.

Taking Mom and Baby Home

Two-day stays in the hospital are generally recommended. Hospitals have been criticized in recent years for trying to discharge new mothers and babies after only one day—so-called "drive-through deliveries." Federal law mandates that your medical insurer pay for forty-eight hours of hospital care after delivery, with the time increased to ninety-six hours for Cesareans. Much of this will depend on your partner. If she feels ready and able to clear out of the hospital, and her doctor says it's okay, take her home.

ESSENTIAL

If you haven't done it already, install the child safety seat in your car. Hospital authorities are not supposed to release children unless the parents have a safety seat in their car, and it is not safe for your partner to hold the baby in her arms while traveling in a moving vehicle. You could stop suddenly or be in an accident, and the child could be in danger.

The actor and comedian Will Smith has a funny bit about driving like a madman to the hospital on the night his wife delivered their baby. But afterward, when he was taking his baby home with him for the first time, he obeys all the traffic laws to the letter and drives as slow and safe as a person can. Not only that, he's yelling out his window at all the crazies on the road who pose a potential threat to his child. It's all a matter of perspective.

And boy, how your perspective has changed! You finally started to understand what this fatherhood thing was all about when you took a moment with your new family after the baby was born. Now you begin the next phase of this most excellent adventure.

CHAPTER 19

Baby Comes Home

When you bought a bassinet, assembled the crib, painted the nursery, and prepared your house, you were getting ready for this very day—the day you get to bring your child home. Despite having done all this, you will quickly discover that you are not prepared at all. This chapter describes how to cope with the arrival of baby and the wild times that are sure to follow.

So What Do We Do Now?

All new parents go through some version of this experience: they've endured nine or so months of pregnancy and a long labor—followed by a satisfying delivery—and finally they bring their baby home with them for the first time. The baby is sleeping, and it is quiet. The parents sit down on the couch together. One of them (often the man) looks at the other and says, "So what do we do now?"

It is indeed a rather humbling thought. You've come so far, traveled all this way, and you really don't know the first thing about raising a child. You turn to your partner expecting her to know the answer, but she just shrugs. She's never had a baby before, either, so how is she supposed to know what to do?

QUOTE

"Starting at birth, read to your child every day," says Carl Guardino, who did this with his children, as often as he could. "It is not only magical bonding time, but studies show that children who are read to every day are more creative, imaginative and do better in school. Invest the time."

Because babies do not talk, so it is often difficult to figure out what they want. What they do, however, is not such a mystery. Babies do five basic things: pee, eat, poop, sleep, and cry.

They can and will do two or more of these things at the same time. They frequently do these things (all but sleep, probably) in the middle of the night, and they may do them several times in the same night. Babies are pee-ing, pooping, crying, eating, and sleeping machines. And they also spit up occasionally.

Terrors: Imaginary and Real

You look with incredibly loving eyes upon your innocent babe, and it is impossible not to occasionally think of all the potential terrors that could befall her. Generally, these terrors exist only in your mind and will never come to pass. Interestingly, too, many of these apparent terrors are not ter-rors at all, but are really quite normal. Your baby may:

- Lose weight after coming home from the hospital.
- Develop jaundice (yellowish skin).
- Seemingly not respond to sounds.
- Have a floppy neck.
- Have a soft spot on her head or a misshapen head.
- Startle abruptly while asleep ("the startle reflex," it is called).

None of these conditions should be taken for granted, but none needs to strike terror in your heart, either. Read up on each condition in case it appears in your child, and get informed about it. The more engaged and knowledgeable you are, the better your partner will feel.

Obviously, your partner also needs to stay in touch with the hospital and go to all the well-baby exams. A well-baby check is basically a physical for your newborn, and the first one takes place within days after she comes home. A good support for your partner is to drive her and baby to the checkup. There, you can ask questions of the pediatrician about anything on your mind.

Some of these conditions, such as a baby losing too much weight too fast, are truly concerning. Other conditions, such as jaundice, may go away with time, although sometimes not. That is why you need to stay involved. Don't be a potted plant at these sessions; speak up and get answers.

Introducing Baby to Your Pet

Bringing your baby home for the first time is a magical moment, although someone in your house may not share in the magic. That someone may be your pet.

Both dogs and cats can come to feel like they own the house they live in. And why not? They've got the run of the place. People let them in and out whenever they wish. These same people feed them and brush them and give them treats. Some animals are even accustomed to sleeping in their owners' beds.

Given all this, it is no wonder that your pet may look askance at this strange new arrival in the house. It may view the child as a potential rival or usurper, and this is actually an accurate assumption. Your cat or dog has, in fact, been replaced as the ruler of the house, so it may be too much of a shock to his system to break this news to him immediately. Let him find out gradually, over time.

Cats

A cat may feel particularly bent out of shape with the arrival of baby. Inevitably, his lap time with Mom and Dad will be severely reduced. In the past, he may have been able to wander freely about the house, but that also has changed.

Keep the cat out of the baby's room. The easiest and most effective way to do this is to keep the door of the room shut while the baby is sleeping or resting in the crib. Some people put netting over the crib to keep the cat out of it. Have your cat sleep in a large cat carrier if you do not want to close the baby's door.

ALERT

Never leave your cat or dog alone in a room with the baby. Nor is it a good idea to put a baby on a blanket with an animal nearby. Even if you are careful, you can never be sure what an animal is going to do. A cat, for example, may want to lie on the blanket too, swatting with its paw if it does not get what it wants.

An old piece of folklore says that cats suck the life out of babies. This tale probably came about when people noticed a cat licking drool from the corner of a baby's mouth. A baby drinks a lot of milk. Her breath and lips smell of milk. The smell of milk may be one reason why cats, who are naturally curious creatures, approach a baby when no one is looking. These approaches are generally harmless, but keeping a cat safely away from a baby is still a good idea.

Dogs

Descended from wolves, dogs are pack animals. Slowly introduce the newest member of your pack to your dog. Let him sniff an article of the baby's clothing after you come home. Dogs have incredible olfactory powers and can pick up a human scent even after the clothing has been washed and dried.

Better still, when Mom and baby are at the hospital, grab a piece of clothing that your child has already worn. Bring it home, and let Fido have a sniff. This way, when baby makes his grand appearance, his scent will already be familiar to your dog.

Supporting Your Family

If you found a way to arrange it with your job and swing it financially, you may be getting ready to spend a week or two with your partner and child. While you may not be on the job during this time, make no mistake about it: this is no vacation. Baby is going to run you ragged.

If you were not able to get some time off after the baby was born and have to go back to work immediately, you will, in effect, have two jobs—the one that pays, and the one that doesn't. Your second, nonpaying job will begin as soon as you get home from your paying one. When you open the door, it may feel like a hurricane hit you. Baby may be screaming and crying, and your partner may be going nuts. Your partner, who may have idealized what it was like to be a Mom and stay home with her newborn, has quickly come to realize what a tough, largely thankless, virtually nonstop job it is. She needs a break, and your job will be to give it to her.

FACT

> Being involved with your children pays off for them as babies and when they are older. Studies have shown that children with involved fathers performed better in school. These children also tend to be socially better adjusted and are far less likely to use drugs and commit crimes.

If you have stayed home with your partner to help her take care of the baby, you may be secretly relieved to go back to your job—the paying one. Not only are you glad to be earning money again, but you're also thrilled at the chance to get some time away from the craziness at home. Indeed, some men feel guilty about leaving their partners to handle the baby while they drive away each morning to work.

But it is useful to remember that the reason fathers work is to support their family. They are working for their families even though they are not in the house. Nowadays, though, more is expected of men than to just supply a paycheck. Be prepared to pitch in and do your share at home. This is another way you can support your family.

The Breastfeeding Challenge

Some men think that women instinctively know how to handle babies. This is not true, of course. Gender alone does not make her an instant expert. She has to learn all this stuff the same way you do—the hard way.

If you need proof of this, wait until she begins to breastfeed the baby. This process may sound easy and even automatic at first—though it is anything but.

You're Involved, Like It or Not

Being a man, your first thought may be, "Well okay, so breastfeeding may be a little tough on her. What does that have to do with me?" In a word, plenty. If she is miserable because the breastfeeding is going so poorly, and the baby is losing weight because she's not getting enough food, that is going to affect you. You are going to be drawn into the middle of this, like it or not.

Her first attempts at breastfeeding will begin in the hospital, as will your first expressions of support for her. The process doesn't end there, not by a long shot. If you want your partner to breastfeed—and physicians do strongly recommend it because breast milk is superior to formula for babies—you will need to continue to offer support, through your words and deeds, in the days and weeks ahead.

A Blow to Their Femininity

For many new mothers, breastfeeding is wrapped up in their sense of themselves as women. Many women expect to breastfeed and eagerly look forward to it. There is something innately female about nursing. Only women can produce milk out of their breasts, from which they can supply food and nourishment to their offspring.

When a new mom encounters difficulties in breastfeeding her baby— and many do—it is sometimes seen as a blow to her femininity. Is there something wrong with her as a woman, as a mother? Your partner may torture herself with questions of this nature. If so, you may see tears of frustration.

In addition, your partner will almost certainly experience physical discomfort from breastfeeding, especially at the beginning when she and the baby are still getting their act together. Her nipples may become chapped and raw.

Getting Some Help

Possibly adding to your partner's woes is her concern for her child. Nearly all babies lose a little weight after they come home from the hospital and before they gradually start putting on the pounds. But your child may not be gaining as much as you think she should. This may throw your partner into a panic and give her more guilt pangs because she fears she is starving her child.

When you only weigh six or seven pounds to begin with, and you're only three or four days old, any weight loss can be a serious business. As with all things having to do with newborns, you need to stay in close touch with your pediatrician or family physician about your baby's weight. Bring the child in to be seen if you have any concerns or questions.

Another thing to do is get some breastfeeding support for your partner. The doctor, your hospital or birthing center, or other mothers may be able to recommend a lactation consultant who can come to your home and give hands-on advice to your partner. There may be a chapter of La Leche League in your town that your partner can hook up with. *"La leche"* is Spanish for "the milk," and the women of La Leche League are all dedicated breastfeeding advocates who will do whatever it takes to help a struggling new mother.

ESSENTIAL

If you and your partner choose to supplement your baby's diet with infant formula, you can, as the child's father, participate in feedings yourself. Giving your baby a bottle will supply her with nourishment, build a bond between the two of you, and provide your partner and her sore breasts with a much-needed break.

Reservations about Breastfeeding

Some men do not want their partner to breastfeed. They worry that the baby's constant tugging on her breasts will make them droop and sag. They want to resume normal lovemaking as soon as they can, and they feel that breastfeeding might somehow get in the way. They may also feel left out of the tight bond formed by a mother and her nursing child.

Some women also do not want to breastfeed. They may not want to in part because their partner has made his feelings known that he doesn't like it. Many women prefer to bottle-feed their babies from the beginning and not worry about things such as their breasts leaking milk. Some people—men and women—are embarrassed by the sight of a woman nursing. They regard it as improper or unseemly.

If you or your partner falls into any of these categories, you still might want to give breastfeeding a try just to see how it works. Even one month of receiving his mother's milk will produce health benefits for your child.

Fathers and Bottle Feeding

It should be stated that there is absolutely nothing wrong with bottle feeding your baby, if that is the choice you make for him. Some mothers simply cannot supply enough food for their hungry baby through breast milk alone, and therefore have to supplement with bottles. Or they may breastfeed during the day and then bottle feed at night to get a chance to sleep.

ALERT

Never warm a bottle of milk in a microwave before feeding it to your baby. Microwaves heat unevenly. While some of the liquid in a bottle may seem fine, there can be hot spots that can scald a baby's throat when he drinks it. Test the warmth of the liquid by shaking a few drops on your wrist. And always check the bottle's nipple so it is not loose inside the ring; if it seems loose, discard it and get a new one.

Bottle feeding is an opportunity for fathers to bond with their children. Some mothers pump their breast milk into bottles (either with a difficult to use hand pump or an expensive electric pump similar to those found in hospitals), or you can use powdered formula. In any case, whereas breast feeding is solely a woman's thing, men can happily share the job of feeding baby with a bottle.

Bottle feeding can certainly be a chore at times, especially if you're walking the floor with your child at three in the morning and you feel like a zombie. But for the most part it is gratifying to give your child what he so desperately wants and needs—food.

It is recommended that you do not put your baby in a crib or bassinet with a bottle or prop him up in a stroller with one. Always hold your baby when you bottle feed him, much the way Moms do when they breastfeed. You gaze with incredible love into your son's eyes while he eats, and then when he is done, you prop his tummy up against your shoulder and give him a firm pat on his back. Then he lets out a grand belch that reminds you proudly of you at your finest.

Fathers and Diapers

Changing diapers is another way to bond with your child—and, let's be honest, an incredible chore as well. You will be amazed at how much your baby poops and pees. The first time you change a diaper, it will seem awkward and you might not do it exactly right. Don't worry. In the next days, weeks, months, and years your baby will give you ample opportunities to perfect your techniques. Before long, you will be the Peyton Manning or Kobe Bryant of changing diapers.

Again, even if you work a job and your partner is tending to baby full-time, do not expect to delegate these responsibilities solely to her. Jump in with both feet and help out. For one, it's the right thing to do. For another, your partner will truly appreciate it. And finally, changing diapers is truly another way to build your relationship with your child.

When she is on her back being changed, you sing her songs. You recite poems to her. You tell her the news of the day. You make faces. She giggles, you giggle. You admire her beautifully chubby body. They are a wonder, these babies and the moments you have with them.

Many men enjoy changing diapers, others not so much. Brian Adams, father of two, falls into the latter category. "Changing diapers is not fun," he says. "But, strange as this sounds, you'll miss changing diapers some day."

Helping Out Around the House

When your partner was pregnant, you probably found yourself doing more chores around the house. Now with the baby at home, you can expect this trend to continue—and then some. You are going to be doing more of everything—changing diapers, possibly bottle feeding the baby, you name it. Even if you go away for eight to ten hours a day to a job, you can expect this. Because as soon as you return home, you will have to pitch in with the baby and everything else that needs to be done.

You and your partner can make yourselves crazy trying to keep an immaculate, Martha-Stewartesque house while caring for the baby, or you can adopt what is called the "Good-Enough Rule." The good-enough rule means exactly that—it's good enough. You can live with it, whatever it is, and that is fine for the moment. If something in the house falls below the good-enough standard, that is when you know you need to focus on it.

The good-enough rule is a survival tactic and a way to keep your sanity. With a newborn in the house, you and your partner are simply not going to be able to devote as much time as you normally do to cooking, cleaning, and other household matters. You need to preserve your energy and mental resources for your number-one job—taking care of your constantly demanding, unrelenting baby.

Caring for Your Child

There are lots of ways to care for your child. One is to go to work, bring home a paycheck, and help support your family financially. Another way to support your child is by supporting your partner since her attention will be focused on the baby. By helping your partner—by encouraging her with breastfeeding, if she chooses to do this, by pitching in with the housework and cooking the meals if you can, by taking the baby for a while so she can get a much-deserved rest—you are helping your child. The bond established between mother and child is the engine that drives early childhood development, and it is a father's job to promote this connection.

Mom Gets in the Way

Assisting your partner, so as to promote the bond between her and her child, is only one part of your job, however. The other part—establishing your own connection—may not be so obvious. Surprisingly perhaps, in many relationships, the person who often interferes with your doing this is your partner.

She is going to spend lots more time with the baby than you are. If she breastfeeds, for example, the baby is going to be with her for long periods off and on throughout the day and night. While she is home with the baby, you are going to be at work. She will likely become the expert in the family on all things related to the baby, such as feeding him, taking him to the doctor, overseeing his nap schedule, and so forth.

ESSENTIAL

One of the chief ways that fathers interact with their children is through play. While children tend to look to their mothers for comfort, they turn to their fathers for stimulation—activity, playfulness, wrestling. Even a baby will respond differently to his mother than his father, becoming more animated in his father's presence.

In addition, whenever she gets the chance and has the energy, she will likely be reading books and magazines about babies and childhood development, visiting parenting websites and blogs, talking to her mother and her friends on the phone, and making connections with other mothers of newborns. She is motivated to learn everything she can because she wants to take good care of her child. All this is wonderful for the most part, but her dominance in all areas having to do with the baby can sometimes nudge the father to the sidelines. This can make him feel like an observer in his own family.

Mom and Dad Interaction

Because Mom is the expert and most familiar with the baby, she sometimes shows little or no patience with Dad, who is not as experienced in putting on diapers or burping the baby and therefore doesn't quite do it right—or at least not the way Mom likes it to be done. Dad feels criticized or inadequate and pulls back from baby-related responsibilities, thus creating a void that Mom needs to fill. She starts doing even more of the baby stuff than she already has been, while Dad goes out to the garage to tinker with his power tools.

Sometimes men are quite happy to abdicate their childrearing responsibilities. Their partner wants to do it? Great. Let her do it. Even if she doesn't want to do it all the time, some men know that their partners will cover for them with the baby if they cut out to go fishing or play golf or shoot some pool after work.

Problems can develop in a relationship, however, if either the man or the woman is continually pushing off the child responsibilities onto the other parent. That vital father-child connection—just as vital, in its way, as the mother-child connection—is going to be weaker and more tentative.

You may need to gently explain to your partner that she can help improve the father-child relationship by taking a well-deserved break now and then. Let the two of you—you and the baby—work things out by yourselves for a while. And really give it a try. If you keep asking her for help when it is your time with the baby, your partner won't learn to relax and let go.

Jobs You Can Do

Taking care of a newborn is not rocket science. It just takes lots of energy and an enduring commitment. When he's hungry, feed him. If he's breast-feeding, hand him to your partner. If his diet needs to be supplemented with formula, give him a bottle. Volunteer to make the formula, always making sure to follow the instructions on the label.

The same with diapers. When a baby's diapers are wet or dirty, change them. When the baby is cranky, pick him up and walk around with him. Sometimes taking him outside into the fresh air can settle him down. A front pack—there are a variety of styles and makes—will hold the baby close to your chest and let you keep your hands free.

At night when the baby cries, get him and bring him back to bed. (Assuming, of course, he is not already in bed with you.) Your partner can feed him from there. If your partner is not breastfeeding, get up and fix the bottle yourself. If he's still cranky, walk him around the living room until he falls asleep.

One of the coolest things you will ever do in your entire life is fall asleep with your newborn in your arms. There is nothing like it in the world. You are on the couch watching the game, and he is lying on your chest, snoozing away. Slowly but surely your eyelids grow heavy, and before you know it, the two of you are sawing logs together. Meanwhile, in another part of the house, your partner is taking a break or resting herself.

Getting Rest

Adequate rest is a must for a newborn. It is also a must for her parents. The trouble is, rest is hard to come by because a newborn may only sleep two to three hours at a time, if that. She is on her own wake-and sleep-schedule, and she couldn't care less about the fact that you have to get up in the morning to go to work.

It is easy to pick out a new father or new mother at the office. New parents look like they haven't had a good night's sleep in weeks because, well, they haven't. Their eyes are bloodshot, their hair is frazzled, and their skin is a sickly pale. They look like zombies because they do what zombies do: stagger around in the dark of night. While the rest of the world sleeps, they are groggily awake, tending to baby.

FACT

In an average day, a working father spends a little under an hour with his children, whereas a working mother spends an hour and twenty minutes. Regardless of whether one works outside the home or not, parents of children six years and younger spend about twice as much time caring for their children than do parents of older kids, for the obvious reason that younger children demand more from their parents.

You and your partner will need to figure out a schedule so that both of you get the rest you need. Maybe she takes most or all of the late night wake-ups during the week, letting you sleep because of your job. Then, maybe before you go to work, you take the baby in the early morning, allowing her to sleep in a little longer. Perhaps you reverse this schedule on the weekends.

You will obviously have more flexibility on the weekends and on your days off. One suggestion might be that you take the baby, say, every Saturday morning. Make it a regular deal. Your partner can sleep in and do whatever she wants. This will provide a boost to her spirits, and give her something to look forward to each week.

Emotional Highs and Lows

Bringing a newborn home for the first time is an emotional moment, causing incredible feelings of happiness and joy. Your home and your life are filled in a way they never were before. You never knew how much you could love a person until you met this child.

Nevertheless, this is also a hectic, emotionally draining, and demanding time. Neither you nor your partner is getting enough rest. The baby is like a dictator and you are her servants, constantly jumping to cater to her every whim and need. You are under a lot of stress and, as a result, you may feel an assortment of emotions other than pure bliss and gratitude.

Postpartum Depression

Your partner may become depressed, seemingly for no reason at all. "Wait a second," you say. "You've got the baby you've always dreamed of. Now you're bummed?" It may not make sense logically, but it still happens with many women, including celebrities such as Brooke Shields. The technical name for it is postpartum depression—commonly known as "the baby blues."

There are a number of reasons for your partner to become depressed. She is almost certainly exhausted. Her back aches. Her breasts are sore and sometimes leak milk. She may feel heavy and sluggish and not like the look of her body right now. On top of all this, she is recovering physically from the heavy rigors of labor and delivery, and this will take months.

Staying home with her newborn may be what she always wanted, but she may find that the reality of it is not what she dreamed of. Caring for a newborn can be isolating, confining, and frustrating. She is always in demand if she is breastfeeding, and she may feel as if she never gets a moment to herself. She may push herself to exhaustion, even as she neglects herself and worries constantly about her baby's well-being and whether or not she is doing the right thing for her child.

But there are some things you can do to help ease her burden. Besides the obvious tasks of diaper changing and helping out more around the house, try one or all of these techniques to lift her spirits (and sometimes yours, too):

- Reassure her frequently that you're in this together, that she's not alone.
- Recruit family and friends to be with her and watch the baby for a while so she can sleep or exercise or whatever.
- Pay for help to come in and lend a hand with the baby or do household chores.
- Encourage her to take walks when she can, get outside in the fresh air, eat well.
- Bring home chocolates or flowers to show her you appreciate her and all she's doing.
- Arrange for a family member to watch the baby, and take her out on a date!

Some communities, churches, and temples have new mom support groups or mom's clubs, and they can ease her sense of isolation. Joining a La Leche League group may be a good step for her as well, since she will meet other women whose experience is similar to hers. She can bring the baby and be social with other Moms with babies.

Most important, you need to stay in tune with what's going on with her, and support her during her down periods. Give her a chance to express her feelings and listen to her. After spending all day with the baby, being able to talk to you—another adult—will be a welcome break.

ALERT

In extreme cases, postpartum depression can be serious. It is possible that your partner may need to see a therapist, who may choose to prescribe medication for her. Some people argue about the value of antidepressants, but one thing is fairly clear: she should avoid taking antidepressants if she is breastfeeding. Generally speaking, whatever she ingests will appear in a diluted form in her breast milk.

Dad's Blues

So Mom is not feeling all that keen, and you know what? To be honest, you've had better days, too. You're feeling just as overwhelmed and just as frazzled. You feel like you're being pulled in all directions at once, with demands coming at you nonstop from the baby, your partner, and your job.

The supportive father and husband is supposed to help out at home, but money is tight and he needs to be on the job. When he's at work, though, he's tired all the time and maybe a little distracted, too. Although he likes to work and wants to be there, he also would like to spend more time with his family. No wonder new fathers get depressed sometimes too.

If you're a new father or about to become one, count on being a little overwhelmed at times. Luckily, the advice for you is the same as it is for your partner. Get rest and exercise. Find a way to take breaks now and then from the many new responsibilities in your life. And get help if you need it.

Think of all you have done and are doing. You have jumped into this completely new experience with both feet, holding the baby, consoling her when she cries, walking her, feeding her, burping her, changing her diapers, and putting her down for a nap. All of this is helping to forge a strong connection between the two of you, which she needs and which is good for you, too. This time you are spending with your child provides a big boost for your partner as well, giving her peace of mind and needed breaks. And, amidst the fatigue and swirling emotions of this time, you are still able to experience, with your new family, moments of pure joy.

Never forget that: it's a crazy time, to be sure, but there is also great joy and happiness.

CHAPTER 20

What's Ahead for You
and Your Family

And so it begins. You and your partner have brought your baby home and somehow survived the first week. But what happens next? What will the next weeks and months bring? This chapter explores the work-family balance, child care, the constant pressures of time and money, and other issues you will face.

Surviving the First Months

In his famous Nobel Prize acceptance speech, novelist William Faulkner said that he believed that man was destined not just to survive, but to prevail. Faulkner was clearly not talking about new parents coping with a baby in the house. Prevail? Fuhgeddaboudit. All you can hope to do is survive.

The first days and weeks and months with a newborn are going to be wild. Oh, come on, let's at least be honest. It is not just a matter of days, weeks, and months. It will take years before you regain the equilibrium you lost when that sweet, innocent, cuddly baby entered your lives and knocked you off your feet.

Because of the demands the baby will make on you, you will have less time for everything. You will get less sleep. You will have less time for yourself. You will have even less sex. Amidst the craziness, though, there will be moments of pure sweetness with your child and your partner. And then, after these amazing, wonderful moments pass, you will return to the general craziness of your life.

The Work-Family Balance

You may have been one of the lucky fathers who was able to take a week or two (or longer) to stay home after the baby was born. You experienced, firsthand, what it was like to take care of a newborn full-time. Thanks to this episode of pure chaos, you felt even luckier to be able to resume your regular schedule and return to the relative sanity of your job.

Immediately, though, a new issue in your life reared its gnarly little head—the work-family balance. You have dealt with this issue before, juggling the demands of work with your desire to spend time with your partner, but that was nothing like this. Having a baby adds a whole new level of stress to the balancing act.

Mom at Home

You and your partner may have decided that, at least for the foreseeable future, she is going to take care of your child full-time. If you can afford it, and your partner is into it, this is a wonderful set-up in so many ways because it is a classic division of labor—one parent largely overseeing the child, the other working a job and bringing home the bacon.

If you are in the latter category (the supplier of bacon), the first thing you will realize is that this arrangement does not absolve you of responsibilities at home. As you will quickly realize, your responsibilities at home have suddenly grown, even though you may be working full-time (and possibly overtime some nights). Welcome to fatherhood, modern style.

ESSENTIAL

> You may call your partner some days and only hear a litany of complaints—how tired she is, how cranky the baby is, how she cannot get five minutes to herself. Let her talk (as much as you can during work) because this will make her feel better. All she may need is to have an adult conversation for a few minutes.

Your partner is devoting herself full-time to the baby. While you may think that this should be enough, and that she should be able to handle all the duties all by herself, it is too much for her alone. She needs your help, and you better to give it to her.

Expect to receive more calls from her while you're at work. Something has come up with the baby, and she needs to talk to you about it. When you call home to check in to see how things are going, you can almost count on her sounding overwhelmed and exhausted. Gradually she will develop a routine and a nap schedule for the baby that allows her to get breaks during the day, but this will take time.

More Demands at Work

While the demands at home have increased with the arrival of a baby, your work schedule has gotten crazier as well. If your work allows it, and you can afford it, you may want to go back to work initially on a part-time basis. Perhaps for a couple of weeks you can find a way to reduce your hours on the job in order to spend more time at home. Most new fathers, however, go back full-time, partly because their employer expects and demands it and partly because they need the money.

Men want and need to be working because that is how they can best support their family at this time. Mom is taking care of baby in the nest, and you're making sure there is a nest for them to be in. Due to the money pressures, many new fathers put in more hours on the job. While this helps out with the finances, it can put a strain on your home life. You may feel torn between being home with your new family and your desire and need to be a success at work.

Exploring Other Options

The man tends to make more money than the woman in most families, but this is not uniformly true. In an increasing number of families today, the woman is the chief bread-winner. This may result in a different sort of family dynamic—one where Mom goes off to work while Dad stays home with the baby.

In the first few months, especially if Mom is breastfeeding, it is going to be hard for her to leave the baby. She is also recovering physically from childbirth, which can take quite a while. But many new mothers can and do return to full-time work as early as six weeks to two months after giving birth.

Stay-at-Home Dad

Economics are the biggest reason that some fathers stay home with their children while their partners work outside the house. Money is not the only reason, however. Lots of men enjoy spending time with their kids and are not averse to the idea of "downsizing" their lives in order to be their children's primary caretaker.

In some families, the couple makes a bargain. If she earns more money, she agrees to work for a period of years to allow him to go back to college or receive more training in his profession. The higher level of training or schooling will give him the opportunity to get a better job with higher pay. When he is ready, he re-enters the job market and returns the favor to his partner. This is certainly not always the case with stay-at-home dads and work-outside-the-house moms, but in some families it just works better that way.

While the number of stay-at-home dads is growing, they are still in the minority. Feeling outnumbered, many stay-at-home dads need to hook up with other men in their situation—if they can find them—and form a support group. This is not a bad idea for new fathers in general. The demands on you at this time are so intense that you may feel the need to talk to other men who are in the same boat you are.

Check out your local hospital or community center; it may sponsor a monthly group session in which new dads get together and bring their babies. Not only do you connect with other men in your position, you get to spend some time with your child. Blogs, online discussion groups, and websites such as those listed in Appendix A of this book are another way in which you can hook up with new fathers, feel solidarity, and form a virtual community.

Child Care

If both you and your partner will be returning to work then the biggest issue you will face is finding child care. In most families, Mom takes the lead in this area, visiting homes or centers and interviewing child care providers to find the right situation. She will need to talk to you about what she has found, and you may need to visit one or two of the places and talk to the people there to help make a final decision.

Basically, there are three options for child care. One is in-home care, in which a nanny or a babysitter comes into your house and watches your child on a one-on-one basis. The second type is family child care, in which your child stays in the home of a licensed provider while you are at work. The third type is a child care center, which is a more formal environment than a person's home and usually has a schedule similar to a preschool. In both child care centers and family child care, the provider will also be supervising other children in addition to your own.

QUOTE

"Child care is a fact of life for most American families," says Nancy Hall, mother of two and an expert on child care issues. "But the care arrangements that families make, even when both parents work outside the home, should not interrupt or interfere with or in any way supplant the love and care of the child's parents for her, nor of the child for her parents."

Many parents rely on family members to help them out with child care. If the baby's grandparents live nearby and are willing to watch your child, that will save you a considerable amount of money. In addition, they may get a charge out of developing a close relationship with their grandchild. When supportive grandparents (or aunts and uncles) do not live nearby, couples will need to find a more permanent solution to the child care issue. Your family will be able to help you out in spots, but you need to find somebody you can count on every day of the workweek.

Overall, your child care provider must be a caring person who is experienced with children and good with them, with the ability and desire to establish a good rapport with your child. She needs to be dependable, safe, clean, well versed in basic first aid and CPR, aware of what to do in an emergency, and be licensed by the state. You and your partner should feel confident that your provider is going to take care of your child as if he were her own.

The Battle for Sleep

Reportedly, one of the most effective means of torturing people is through sleep deprivation. This method is used, for instance, by combatants during wartime. To obtain information from a reluctant-to-talk prisoner of war, interrogators change and disrupt his sleep schedule, turning day into night and night into day. He becomes disoriented and more dependent on his captors and, it is thought, more willing to spill the beans to them.

As the father of a newborn, you may feel a little like a prisoner of war being subjected to sleep deprivation techniques. You stagger around bleary-eyed and yawning uncontrollably. By the middle of the afternoon you feel like crawling under your desk or escaping to your car for a long nap. Sleep for a new father is like sex—you are simply not going to get nearly enough of it in the early days after the baby is born.

Baby's Sleep Schedule

One of your prime goals as a new parent will be to get your baby on the same sleep schedule as you. In other words, you want her to sleep through the night with no wake-ups. Realistically, though, you and your partner may have to endure many sleep-interrupted nights before your child reaches this point.

Some babies begin to sleep through the night almost immediately. You always hate to talk to these parents if you are a new parent and your child wakes up frequently because it is impossible not to feel jealous. These people are bright-eyed and have lots of energy, while you're struggling to keep your eyes open after having woken three times in the middle of the night by your squalling baby.

Nevertheless, you ask them how they did it—how they achieved this miracle of a baby sleeping through the night—and they tell you what works for them. Unfortunately, what worked for them may not work for you. Here are some of the issues that are involved in teaching a baby to sleep through the night:

- The age of the baby
- Her daily routine
- When she takes her naps
- How long her naps are
- What the baby eats, and how often
- Where the baby sleeps (in her bed or with parents)
- Whether her parents help her to sleep by rocking or other methods

Generally, by about six months babies begin to sleep through the night, if not sooner. But every child is different. As with so many things having to do with babies, much of this depends on the child. Some babies sleep as contentedly as cats, while others are more restless and stir more often.

ESSENTIAL

Keeping a consistent routine is a vital ingredient in helping teach your baby how to sleep through the night. She needs to do basically the same things at roughly the same time each day. This includes her nighttime schedule. Habit and routine can help teach her when it is time to go to sleep.

Your Sleep Schedule (and Your Partner's)

Doctors and parenting experts like to advise new parents to sleep when their baby sleeps. If the baby is only sleeping for two hours at a time, be sure to grab some rest at those times. Once the baby wakes up, you are going to be in demand again. If you do not rest when you get the chance, you are going to drive yourself to exhaustion and possibly depression.

Your best ally in this regard is your partner, just as you are her best ally. Find an arrangement that works for both of you. If you have to get up in the morning to go to work, let her take the night shift with the baby during the week. On the weekends, reverse roles. You need to exchange baby watching duties so each of you can get breaks and sleep.

If you need to work and cannot get the sleep you need, you may want to consider staying one night a week at a friend's or your parents' house, if they live nearby. Your overtired partner may also want to consider doing the same—just to get a good night's rest.

Time and Money Pressures

Parents of newborns are under a lot of pressure. The needs of the baby are nearly constant. He is vulnerable and helpless and cannot use words yet to tell you what he likes or dislikes. Sometimes he gets sick and needs to go to the doctor. Meanwhile, you must deal with the worries and handle all the responsibilities while you're feeling stressed and worn out from a lack of sleep.

Adding to these pressures are those two old regulars, not enough money and not enough time. You never had enough money or time before and now, with a child, your wallet and calendar seem stretched almost to the breaking point. To find a way to handle all your added responsibilities, you will likely need to cut back temporarily on certain things you used to do regularly, such as getting together with the guys after work. When life takes on a more normal shape again, you can resume those activities.

As long as you have a young child (or children), there will be demands on your time and wallet. If you can, though, take a longer view. Gradually, the seemingly overwhelming responsibilities that you currently feel will ease up. The yoke will lighten. The first year of your baby's life is probably the most harried you will ever feel as a parent. Rest assured that one of these days, you will get your life back.

You and Your Partner

It's a fact, babies put stress on a relationship. You will not have as much time with your partner as you used to. When you do find time to be together without the baby, you will be tired and stressed from all your other responsibilities.

Nevertheless, you need to find ways to keep your relationship with your partner alive and vibrant. That does not necessarily mean taking weeklong romantic getaways to the Caribbean or Hawaii, although those are nice. Rather, it means making small connections with your partner every day. That might mean:

- Walking together with the baby.
- Talking about the baby, but not *only* about the baby.
- Going shopping or doing other mundane errands together, just to spend time with your partner.
- Holding her hand or rubbing her shoulders, for no specific reason.
- Surprising her with flowers or a gift.
- Going on a date (without the baby) from time to time.
- Cuddling in bed at the end of the day.

Rest assured: sex will return. Not right away—it will take at least six weeks after the baby is born, and probably longer, before your partner is ready. She may not be physically up to it, depending on whether or not there was tearing during childbirth or if she delivered through a C-section or some other complication. It takes time to heal. But gradually, as your partner begins to feel better physically and emotionally, you will be able to rediscover this side of your relationship.

ALERT

Don't push too hard on the sex issue; no need to rush. Things will take their natural course, and gradually your partner's lust for your studly body will return. It takes a long time for many new mothers to feel interested in sex after giving birth, partly because they can't fully relax in their still-recuperating bodies. Be a man with a slow hand, as the song goes, and you will be better off.

You and Your Baby

The same advice applies to your relationship with your child as well—take it slow. You've got your whole life to get to know this child. Don't feel bad if for some reason you do not feel totally connected to your child the moment he is born.

Some parents expect to fall immediately and completely in love with their child the instant they lay eyes on him. This certainly does occur, but love usually acts less like a lightning bolt and more like a plant. It takes time and care and nurturing to blossom.

QUOTE

Bob Kaehms, the father of three, realizes that it is inevitable that fathers (and mothers) get their egos wrapped up in their children. But he recommends restraint in this regard: "Don't live or re-live your dreams through your children, but help them find their dreams, and support them." Not bad advice as the days and months and years roll on.

It's Mom's Show in the Beginning

In the early days and months of having a baby, it is basically Mom's show. Now that does not mean that dear old Dad cannot contribute; of course he can. He can do all the things that Mom does with the baby (except breast-feed, of course), while building his own close relationship with his child.

Having said that, the point still stands. This early time with the baby, with some exceptions, is basically Mom's show. When the baby needs to eat, Mom will mainly feed him. When he needs to settle down, Mom will mainly take him and put him down. She bore this child with her own body, and she will act as primary caretaker for him in his tender years.

FACT

Men define success in a variety of ways. This might include making money, achieving recognition in their work, earning the admiration of their peers, or having a loving relationship with a woman. But nearly 90 percent of all men say that being a good father is a vital part of a successful life.

Your Time Is Coming

Most new fathers do not dispute these facts or seek to overturn them. They like the fact that Mom is in charge of the baby. They consider that their principal job is to be good helpers—helping their partners, helping to take care of their children, and helping to create an environment in which Mom and baby feel protected and safe.

As a new father, one thing you can look forward to is the future; it keeps getting better. Every day the baby gets older, it gets better for you. The baby grows stronger and livelier and is more able to interact with you—daily, he is emerging from his larva-like state and becoming more of an emerging butterfly. This will give both of you more and more chances to enjoy each other's company.

Suggested Reading for New Fathers and Fathers-to-Be

Ash, Jennifer and Armin Brott. *Expectant and First-Year Father, Second Edition.* (New York: Abbeville Press, 2004).

Two-book set for fathers-to-be and new fathers full of useful facts, tips, and advice.

Barry, Dave. *Babies and Other Hazards of Sex: How to Make a Tiny Person in Only 9 Months, With Tools You Probably have around the Home* (Emmaus, PA: Rodale Books, 2000).

Timeless humor from the Pulitzer Prize-winning columnist and father.

Eisenberg, Arlene, with Sandee Hathaway and Heidi Murkoff. *What to Expect When You're Expecting.* Fourth Edition (New York: Workman Publishing, 2008).

This best-selling, comprehensive guide to pregnancy is oriented mainly toward women, but there is a useful section for fathers called "Fathers Are Expectant, Too."

Iannelli, Vincent, MD. *The Everything® Father's First Year Book: A Survival Guide for the First 12 Months of Being a Dad* (Avon, MA: Adams Media, 2005).

A companion book to this volume, for fathers in baby's first year.

Nilsson, Lennart. *A Child Is Born.* (New York: Bantam Doubleday, 2004).

A revised and updated reissue of the classic photography book that depicts the growth of an embryo and fetus within the womb, and the miracle of birth. These extraordinary pictures may help fathers-to-be better visualize and feel more connected to what is going on inside their partners.

Sears, James M. and Robert W. Sears. *Father's First Steps: 25 Things Every New Dad Should Know* (Boston: Harvard Press, 2006).

A primer on fathering from two pediatricians and fathers, the sons of renowned baby doctor Dr. William Sears.

APPENDIX B

Online Resources

Ask Dr. Sears

Medical and other parenting advice for parents and fathers by pediatricians.
www.askdrsears.com

Dadlabs.com

Videos and humor for fathers.
www.dadlabs.com

Daddytude

An often humorous blog about being a father.
www.daddytude.com

Fatherhood.org

Blogs, communities, clubs, and resources for fathers both new and old.
www.fatherhood.org

Fathering Magazine

Articles, stories, poems on "man's most important work."
www.fathermag.com

Fatherville

Fathers writing about fatherhood: blogs, articles, and discussion groups.
www.fatherville.com

I'm Going to be a Dad

Weekly pregnancy e-guides for men: facts, tips, ideas, and more.
www.imgoingtobeadad.com.au

Mrdad.com

Information for new and expectant fathers, with links to an array of sites and resources for fathers.
www.mrdad.com

Web MD

Another respected medical site with information on parenting and pregnancy.
www.webmd.com

Index

Find out Everything on Anything at **everything.com!**

The new **Everything.com** has answers to your questions on just about everything! Based on the bestselling Everything book series, the **Everything.com** community provides a unique connection between members and experts in a variety of fields. Since 1996, Everything experts have helped millions of readers learn something new in an easy-to-understand, accessible, and fun way. And now Everything advice and know-how is available online.

At **Everything.com** you can explore thousands of articles on hundreds of topics—from starting your own business and personal finance to health-care advice and help with parenting, cooking, learning a new language, and more. And you also can:

- **Share advice**
- **Rate articles**
- **Submit articles**
- **Sign up for our Everything.com newsletters to stay informed of the latest articles, areas of interest, exciting sweepstakes, and more!**

Visit **Everything.com** where you'll find the broadest range and most authoritative content available online!